© 2007 Don Taylor

About the Author

STEPHEN M. YOUNGER, PH.D., is a senior policy scholar at the
Woodrow Wilson International Center for Scholars. He is a former senior fellow at Los Alamos National Laboratory, where he
previously was in charge of nuclear weapons research and development. From 2001 to 2004, he was director of the Defense
Threat Reduction Agency at the U.S. Department of Defense.
He lives in Las Vegas.

endangered species

AN BOOK

HARPER ⬤ PERENNIAL

NEW YORK • LONDON • TORONTO • SYDNEY • NEW DELHI • AUCKLAND

endangered species

HOW WE CAN AVOID

MASS DESTRUCTION AND

BUILD A LASTING PEACE

stephen m. younger

HARPER ● PERENNIAL

A hardcover edition of this book was published in 2007 by Ecco, an imprint of HarperCollins Publishers.

FIRST HARPER PERENNIAL EDITION PUBLISHED 2008.

Designed by Cassandra J. Pappas

The Library of Congress has catalogued the hardcover edition as follows:

Younger, Stephen Michael.
    Endangered species : how we can avoid mass destruction and build a lasting peace / Stephen M. Younger.—1st ed.
        p.   cm.
        ISBN: 978-0-06-113951-2
        ISBN-10: 0-06-113951-3
    1. Violence. 2. War. 3. Terrorism. 4. Weapons of mass destruction. 5. Violence—Prevention. 6. Conflict management. 7. Peace. 8. Civilization, Modern—21st century. I. Title.

HM886.Y68 2007
303.6—dc22   2006048163

ISBN 978-0-06-113952-9 (pbk.)

08 09 10 11 12 BVG/RRD 10 9 8 7 6 5 4 3 2 1

For Mari, James, and Joel

contents

acknowledgments

It is appropriate that a book on preventing mass violence was written at the Woodrow Wilson International Center for Scholars. This remarkable institution, located just a few blocks from the White House in Washington, D.C., is a meeting ground for scholars and policy makers and a living memorial to President Woodrow Wilson's vision of peace. I would especially like to thank Director Lee Hamilton for my appointment as a senior policy scholar and Robert Litwak and Kent Hughes for many helpful and illuminating conversations. I am very grateful to Joseph Brinley for key editorial advice early in my writing. Jane Mutnick provided administrative support during my visits to the center.

During the years that I planned to write this book, I spoke with scores of people and received the benefit of much knowledge and wisdom. I would especially like to thank James Schlesinger for several helpful conversations and John Browne for encouraging the project at an early stage. Bradley Roberts directed me to several useful references in political science and the theory of conflict. David Sharp and Rajan Gupta patiently listened to my development of the themes of the book and offered many helpful suggestions. I would especially like to thank my wife, Mari, for a careful reading of the manuscript and many valuable comments.

After a career spent in national security, I was fairly confident in my views on the nature of violence and its probable future. Glenn Paige and Leslie Sponsel challenged those views and encouraged me to look deeper at the curious traits of our species. To both of these men, I owe a profound debt of gratitude.

My thinking on the proliferation of weapons of mass destruction was refined during my tenure as director of the Defense Threat Reduction Agency in the U.S. Department of Defense. I would like to thank all of my colleagues at DTRA for helping me to understand the need for a global view of the future threat and the importance of engaging all of the tools at our disposal.

It is a pleasure to thank my literary agents, Donald Lamm and Christy Fletcher, for many suggestions and for their encouragement in the completion of this project. Emily Takoudes, my editor at Ecco, guided me through the publication process and provided several important insights.

preface

The world is at a crossroads. For the first time, we face a set of challenges that will determine our future not only as nationalities or ethnic groups but as a species. Rarely does a society cross a fundamental threshold, one in which things are demonstrably different on the other side. Today we are crossing two.

The ability to cause mass destruction—more than 100,000 deaths—is spreading from nation-states to small groups and even individuals. Fifty years ago it took an invading army or massive aerial bombardment to cause such carnage, but today the same effect can be caused by a single nuclear, chemical, or biological weapon, tools of destruction that are becoming available to more and more countries and even to terrorist organizations. No longer will our future be determined by the small number of countries with the wealth and resources to support large armed forces. Any organization that wants the tools of mass destruction will have them.

The second threshold that we have *already* crossed is that the pace of world events has exceeded the capacity of a human brain to think about them. A single individual with a computer can reach a billion people before responsible governments even know that it's happening. Ballistic missiles can carry weapons across the globe in less than an hour.

Combined, these two thresholds make for a deadly cocktail. We can no longer afford to wait for a crisis before we take action. The widening availability of destructive technologies and the speed with which they can be used makes it imperative that we address the causes and motivations for *all* forms of organized violence, from terrorism to international wars. We must wage war on war itself.

This is a book about investing in our future. It does not pine for Utopia, the best possible world, but attempts to lay out a program for achieving the best practical world consistent with human nature. It looks at the root causes of mass violence and proposes concrete measures that can be used to address those causes. Democracy must be spread to even more countries to give people hope for their future. Economic tools must focus on alleviating inequities that lead to genocide and war. And, as a last resort, military capability must be designed not only to win wars but to win peace.

Never have we faced greater danger. And never have we had better tools to deal with that danger. As with poverty, disease, and hunger, the threat of mass violence will not go away unless we make it go away, applying the same degree of determination as in any other urgent priority. We are an imperfect species, but a gifted one. The choice is ours.

endangered species

|| **the imperative for change**

The only thing necessary for the triumph of
evil is for good men to do nothing.

—EDMUND BURKE

The crater was only about 500 feet across and 50 feet deep; there
were certainly bigger ones at the Nevada Test Site. What was special
about this one was that it was *my* crater, made with the first nuclear
explosive that I had designed on my own. What had started as a pencil sketch eighteen months before ended in a fireball hotter than the
surface of the sun, an energy pulse that vaporized thousands of tons
of rock to create a huge bubble over a thousand feet below the desert
floor. As this artificial cavern cooled, its roof collapsed and rock and
sand cascaded downward until, when there was no more rock to fall,
a crater formed on the surface.

I walked up to the edge, careful not to trip over the many fissures
that had been opened by the intense shock waves. The air was filled
with the roar of electrical generators that powered measuring equipment in trailers. All about me people moved purposefully and according to plan, some recovering film from the scores of cameras
attached to oscilloscopes, some monitoring possible radiation leaks

(there were none), and some preparing to move heavy equipment needed for upcoming tests. There was a sense of accomplishment, of having done something that was important and having done it well.

Standing at the edge of that crater, my mind was busy trying to connect what I was looking at with the work that I had done on the device that had created it. I went over the whole process—the hundreds of hours spent on computer calculations, the graphs that predicted the implosion, the machines that were used to fashion its components, the sputter of the welder as it bound those parts together. Until that moment I thought I knew every minute detail of the device, but it was only when I stood on the edge of my crater that the essence of nuclear weapons came home to me. It was only then that I understood in my heart as well as my mind the magnitude of destruction that could be caused by nuclear explosions. Although I did not realize it at the time, that nuclear test in 1983 was a personal transformation, an experience that started a train of thought which ultimately led to this book.

I have been in the nuclear weapons business for over twenty years and I have always been a pacifist. I have designed and tested devices that produce the biggest bang in the world, yet I don't like loud noises. I have argued for the development of the most destructive weapons ever created, yet I dislike violence in any form. I don't watch violent movies and I don't read violent thrillers. I have held a gun twice and I don't ever intend to own one. I also understand that not everyone shares the same revulsion for killing that I do. For all of our progress, for all of our civility, the world still harbors those who would plunder and kill for personal gain, for the glory of their country, or just to satisfy a primal lust to destroy. I may be a pacifist, but I am not stupid—5,000 years of history have taught me that another word for an unarmed country is "target."

There was euphoria at the end of the cold war, a great sigh of relief when we realized that the danger of mutually assured destruction had passed. The threat of global Armageddon was leaving with the twentieth century, by far the bloodiest of our long and troubled history. We talked about entering a new age. Lacking any better title, we called it the "post–cold war period." There would be a huge "peace dividend" wherein some of the billions spent on weapons could be redirected to urgent social problems. Instead of guns, we would buy schoolbooks, instead of aircraft carriers, we would build hospitals; the budget deficit would be reduced and everyone would be better off. And it wasn't just in the United States. Who can forget watching television images of the jubilant crowds in Berlin tearing down the Wall? Or the "velvet revolution" when a poet was elected president of Czechoslovakia, a country that had for so long suffered under the heel of communism? It was the triumph of democracy over tyranny, a new beginning for all of us. It was not to last.

Fifteen years later, the United States is embroiled in a global war against terrorism with hundreds of thousands of troops fighting in Iraq and Afghanistan. We are told that this war may last years, even generations, and that we must be ready to sacrifice our blood and our treasure to win it. We may have to accept limits on our personal freedom to assure that freedom. The budget surplus that we all dreamed of spending has turned into a record deficit. In 1989, the United States was seen as the great liberator, the country that, through a combination of strength and patience, had defeated the "Evil Empire" and ushered in a new era of peace and democracy. By early 2004, a majority of the populations of our closest allies thought that the *United States* was the greatest threat to world security, that our unilateral approach to international politics had gone too far, that we were causing problems rather than solving them.

What happened? September 11, 2001. Airplanes crashing into the twin towers of the World Trade Center, people jumping from windows, bodies being carried from the Pentagon, weeping firemen in Pennsylvania—these terrible images were burned into our collective memory. None of us will ever forget that day. Ironically, I had arrived in Washington, D.C., only the week before to serve as director of the Defense Threat Reduction Agency, an organization designed to reduce the threat of weapons of mass destruction. My mind was focused on programs to dismantle Russian nuclear submarines, destroy the remaining American chemical weapons, and find better ways to deal with an attack involving biological weapons. It was to be a safer future, and I was there to make it happen.

But as I watched the terrible events unfold on the television in my office at Fort Belvoir, I knew that we had entered into a new and frightening world. Slowly my senior staff, which was half military and half civilian, wandered into my office. Colonel Ronnie Faircloth, my chief of staff, reported that the threat condition in the Washington area had been raised to delta: the nation was under attack. We wondered when last this had happened. Pearl Harbor perhaps? We discussed arming the soldiers assigned to the agency to defend against terrorist attacks since no one knew when or where the violence would stop. (I decided not to, thinking that the risk of nervous people armed with automatic weapons was greater than the threat of an attack on our offices. And, despite being a defense agency, we didn't have many guns to pass around.) Technical groups swung into action to model wind patterns around the impact sites; there was a worry that the planes could have carried deadly chemicals or even biological weapons, making the attack even more insidious. But most of all we wondered, as did all Americans, how was it possible that the capital of the most powerful nation in the world was under attack?

Within days we knew who had done it. This didn't take brilliant detective work since the leaders of the plot went on television to brag about their success. Even more disturbing, we watched news reports of Arab crowds celebrating the attack as a great victory against the West; we got what was coming to us, they said, a comeuppance for years of arrogance. People were selling Osama bin Laden T-shirts on Egyptian street corners and there was a rush to name Muslim babies Osama.

Conversely, American embassies around the world were barricaded by mounds of flowers left in sympathy. A German destroyer engaged in NATO exercises in the North Atlantic signaled for permission to do a close approach to one of our ships, the USS *Winston Churchill*. As it passed, the American crew saw the stars and stripes flying from the mast. The German crew lined the rail in dress uniforms holding a banner that read, "We are with you." I am told that there was not a dry eye on the *Churchill*'s bridge.

The United States went to war. It was more than revenge for New York, Washington, and Pennsylvania. It was a reasoned counterattack against those who would threaten the very foundation of our civilization, those who rejected the idea of freedom that is so precious to every American citizen, those who saw little value in human life as they attempted to turn a third of the world into a religious dictatorship. These were people who saw democracy as an affront to God, the usurping of divine power in favor of the lowest common denominator of popular opinion. It was not a case of if they knew us they would love us. They knew us and they hated us with murderous passion.

What changed? Not terrorism—just think of Northern Ireland, the bombing in Oklahoma City, the bombs exploded outside American embassies in Africa. There was also the attack on the USS *Cole* when a speedboat loaded with explosives blew a hole the size of a truck in the side of the ship. And the previous bombing of the World Trade Center. Think of the number of wars around the world, including the many instances of genocide, one of which is occurring in Darfur even as I write these words. We have been killing one another for thousands of years and somehow our species has managed to survive—even the worst wars killed only a small fraction of the world's population. A few historians have gone so far as to argue that wars were effective means of population control and that the same number of deaths would have occurred by starvation if not by violence. After all, we are only human, an imperfect species. While the path of progress has hardly been straight, we do seem to be making steady improvements. Many deadly diseases have been eradicated from the planet and there is an overall rise in life expectancy, even in the poorest countries. We are eternal optimists; we'll win the war against global terrorism and once again life will be good.

Maybe not. While we hunt for terrorists and try to instill order in Iraq, other changes are afoot that will make the future far more dangerous than anything we have ever faced. We are about to cross two thresholds that will have a profound effect on how we think about ourselves and the world around us. They make a deadly pairing that, in a species which has all too often been willing to use violence to achieve its objectives, should ring alarms in every nation in the world. Consider the following:

- The ability to cause mass destruction is spreading from the domain of the major nation to the domain of a small country, group, or even an individual.

- The speed with which information, people, and weapons can move around the world is exceeding the ability of a human being to think about and respond to unfolding events.

In combination, these thresholds point to a time when events can easily get out of control and lead to history-changing consequences.

Fifty years ago, it took the resources of a major country to kill 100,000 people. Excluding natural events such as earthquakes and epidemics, this level of carnage was the domain of state-sponsored war or genocide, limited to a relatively small number of nations. At the beginning of World War II, it took an invading army or a massive bombing raid to cause 100,000 deaths, a capability that cost billions of dollars and one that only a few nations could afford. The atomic bomb raised the potential death toll of an attack from thousands to millions, but the tools of mass destruction were still owned by only a few countries, all of which knew that any use of these ultimate weapons would result in an immediate response in kind. During the cold war, the United States and the Soviet Union developed an elaborate set of rules for how countries behaved, rules that were usually obeyed by both sides since neither wanted to risk a nuclear cataclysm. Wars were local and contained, tragic in their own right, but usually not a threat to our national survival.

Today, we're confronted by fanatics who believe that they have been ordered by God to kill as many Westerners as possible, fanatics who are seeking the means to murder on a massive scale. Terrorists think that by attacking innocent civilians they can force governments to accept their demands. Osama bin Laden has vowed to kill 4 million Americans, half of them children. Fifty years ago—even ten years ago—this would have been an idle threat, impossible for anyone to do without the backing of a major nation. Today, every civilized country in the world worries about terrorists stealing a nuclear weapon or having one willingly provided by a sympathetic government. And it does not take a nuclear weapon to cause one hundred thousand deaths. There are easier ways.

Imagine the following. A bright young man comes to the United States to study. He is the first of his family to attend a university, let alone travel across the ocean to live in a different country—the pride of his town, a delight to his parents, the poor boy who made good. He does well in school and goes on to get a Ph.D. in molecular biology in hopes of creating a new generation of drugs that will ease the suffering of people in the poorer parts of the world. But over time, he becomes homesick; despite all of the comforts of the West, he misses his family and the culture in which he was raised. He starts to attend a local mosque, where he hears sermons about the excesses of the West and the erosion of traditional Islamic values around the world. How many people just like him were killed by war or disease while Western nations, particularly the United States, stole their natural resources and walked away? Gradually, our bright young scientist is drawn into the terrorist fold, until one day he is given the order to use his skills to launch an unprecedented attack on the Great Satan.

He rents office space in a high-tech business park in greater Los Angeles, starts a phony company, and searches the Internet for used equipment that he can get at bargain prices. Within a few weeks, he has everything that he needs to develop a virus. Using his training in molecular biology, he modifies the virus's structure to a form that is resistant to any known treatment. He tries out his creation on some laboratory animals. After some false starts he settles on a particularly deadly candidate and begins small-scale manufacture. It only takes a few weeks to grow a kilogram of the agent, easy to fit into a lunch box.

Where should he attack? Where can he count on finding the greatest number of people who can be infected with the virus? Why not choose several places—an airport, a convention center, and a crowded intersection in downtown LA? Battery-powered sprayers are constructed and hidden inside briefcases; willing volunteers are recruited from a clandestine network of terrorist cells. Finally, on a beautiful California morning four well-dressed young men carry their briefcases to two domestic terminals at LAX, a downtown technology expo, and the corner of Hollywood and Vine. No one notices the practically invisible spray coming from a tiny hole drilled into the side of each case, a spray that carries a disease that did not exist until it was created for the sole purpose of killing. Some of those who are exposed board airplanes, carrying the germs to other parts of the country.

A week later, physicians and hospitals begin seeing large numbers of people with illnesses that look somewhat like the flu but with a curious twist. The patients have difficulty breathing and there is some internal bleeding; it's nothing quite like what doctors have seen before. None of the usual treatments seem to work and, after a few days, the weakest of the victims, infants and the elderly, begin to die. Other cities report outbreaks and experts at the Centers for Disease Control in Atlanta are called in to investigate. Scientists quickly isolate the virus and catalog it as something new; most frightening, it is something created by human beings rather than by the natural mutation of an existing disease. Laboratories around the world search for an effective treatment. Nothing on the shelf works, but the virus is similar enough to what has been seen before that it should be possible to adjust an existing medicine to fight it. The usual requirements for testing and certification are waived and mass immunizations begin within sixty days. A few months later, the epidemic dies out as a result of its own efficiency at killing and the effect of public treatment. One million people have died.

If you think that this is too difficult to pull off, that someone would notice suspicious activities in a secretive start-up company, try this scenario: At midnight, three terrorists sit in a parked minivan next to a rail yard in downtown Philadelphia. They watch the trains go by until they see their quarry, a string of ten jet-black tank cars with hazardous-material signs affixed to their sides. The cars are being switched from one freight train to another and, for a short time, will be left alone. It takes about five minutes for the three men to leave their vehicle, walk along the track, and hide small packages on each of the tank cars. Soon they are back in their van, heading out of town, long gone when a series of small explosions rupture the walls of each of the tank cars, spilling hundreds of tons of industrial phosgene onto the ground. Like liquefied natural gas, the phosgene rapidly evaporates and, being heavier than the surrounding air, it hugs the surface. Winds spread the clouds toward the downtown area. Railroad personnel responding to the explosions clutch their throats and collapse. Firemen arrive but are powerless to contain the spread of the gas; all they can do is watch the green cloud move toward the city where hundreds of thousands of people are sleeping peacefully.

The Philadelphia emergency response unit is notified and, within minutes of the initial report, every radio and television station is broadcasting an urgent order to evacuate. Take nothing, don't wait to lock up, get out now and head north as fast as possible. If you can't move, then go to a windowless room and use the duct tape that you bought a few years ago to seal the door and any air vents; stay put until you hear the all clear on the radio. Police cars drive up and down streets, sirens blaring to wake sleeping residents; only a few night owls actually hear the broadcasts. By the time people are awake and moving, the cloud is upon them. Within an hour, over two hundred thousand people are dead. Five hundred thousand more are in need of treatment, but the hospitals themselves are barely recovering from the attack and there are not nearly enough doctors, nurses, and equipment to deal with even the most urgent cases.

We try to convince ourselves that we can win the war against terrorism. And when it's over we'll resume the traditional international relations that we're comfortable with, dealing with rational governments who know that they can't expect to attack the United States and get away with it. Here, too, we are in for a rude awakening, for it is not only terrorism that presents a new threat to our future. Fifty years ago only two countries, the United States and Russia, had the technological wherewithal to construct a nuclear weapon. Today, Great Britain, France, China, India, Pakistan, and Israel have joined the nuclear club and half a dozen other countries are believed to be pursuing their own nuclear programs. Scientists in Pakistan went so far as to sell do-it-yourself kits to almost any country with the cash and interest to create their own nuclear materials enrichment capability. There are good reasons to believe that North Korea and Iran were eager customers. For additional money, the Pakistanis would sell blueprints for a crude but workable bomb. Equally entrepreneurial salesmen in North Korea offered a long-range missile to carry the weapon. Or you could just put the bomb in a shipping container with a consignment of baby clothes and send it COD, arranging for it to go off when the container was opened for inspection or unloading at a Western port. Weapons that were once the sole domain of a superpower are now within reach of almost any country with a rudimentary technological capability and a stable supply of electricity. Even the smallest of countries will soon be able to carry a big stick.

These are not outrageous stories. Each one is more than plausible and represents a threat that has been validated in numerous U.S. government studies. They demonstrate that the comfortable security that we have enjoyed, a security based on our conventional military superiority, is about to disappear. We can't expect to invade every country that we suspect of developing nuclear weapons. Tanks and aircraft carriers cannot stop terrorists who are willing to give their lives for their cause and exploit the freedoms of civilized nations to attack them in the most heinous manner. We face a new set of determined adversaries, adversaries with the capability to cause death and destruction on a scale hitherto the domain of powerful nations. Time has run out on our complacency; the pace of events is accelerating. Advances in communications and transportation are giving terrorists the ability to reach hundreds of millions of people faster than we can analyze what's happening.

The human brain is a marvelous object, the enabler of the civilization that has transformed our planet and allowed us to take our first faltering steps out into the solar system. It is, however, a biological machine that works at its own pace. Think about the last time you were involved in a traffic accident, when someone close to you died, or when you were told that you had to have a life-saving operation. You were in shock; your whole view of the world collapsed into that one traumatic event. It was only after some hours—eight to twelve for most people—that you were able to regain perspective, to think about other things beyond calling the insurance company, talking to the funeral director, or preparing to go to the hospital. You talked with friends and loved ones, going over the problem again and again until you were better able to understand it. Some people take walks, some have a drink, others pray; everyone has their own way of dealing with life's events. In every case, however, *time* is one of the principal ingredients. Now, with the astonishing rise in the speed of communications and transportation, history-changing events can happen faster than we can think about them. We don't have eight to twelve hours to think things through, to get wise counsel, to weigh responses and consider options—in that time the world could turn into a very different place.

Twenty years ago it took hours or days for information to spread around the world. Only governments and major news organizations had the ability to broadcast news by radio, television, or newspaper to millions of people. Except for extraordinary events like assassinations or natural catastrophes, most people received information about world events from the morning paper or the evening news. Today, a single individual with no more investment than a personal computer and a telephone line can reach billions of people worldwide, potentially stirring up discontent or violence faster than responsible governments can think about responding. Terrorists issue proclamations and show the grisly results of their violence using their own websites that are completely separate from any government or news organization. Anyone with a computer and access to the Internet can hear what an organization halfway around the world has to say, sometimes quite literally by watching streaming video. It is nearly impossible for governments to suppress such sources of information. Instead of people turning to a few responsible sources for an interpretation of unfolding events, they are choosing their own authority figures.

It is not only that things are happening faster every day; they are happening faster than our mental ability to keep track of them. We simply can't respond fast enough to so many things happening at once. News creates its own news and, moving at the speed of light, it can go through several mutations before governments can do more than scramble a hurried response. What transforms this acceleration of events into a threshold in world affairs is that it is surpassing a fundamental limit, the ability of our own human minds to assimilate and make sense of new, and in many cases shocking, information. The pace of events demands that we do much more work up front to plan for even remote contingencies. We can no longer muddle through, making up our response as we go along or, worse, risk being led down a path not of our choosing.

My generation, born in the mid–twentieth century, was the first that thought nothing of relocating for work or simply because we wanted to live elsewhere. We live in a society that is becoming more mobile every day. My son lives in Australia. When I asked him if he intends to remain there, he said he didn't know, and that, after all, it was only a plane ride from home. Whereas my generation was the first to think nothing of moving to a different part of the country, his is the first to think little of moving to a different part of the world. It can cost less to buy an airline ticket from Washington to London than from Washington to Cincinnati. It is cheaper to ship parts from the United States to China for assembly, paying transportation costs both ways, than it is to put the final product together here. We are annoyed when an international package from Tokyo takes more than a day to arrive at our doorstep.

Twenty years ago about half the world's population lived in relative isolation. Hundreds of millions of people in countries like India and China farmed and tended animals in the countryside, much as their ancestors had done for hundreds, if not thousands, of years.

They were pretty much on their own, raising their children, occasionally visiting medical clinics when they could be reached on foot
or by an occasional rickety bus. They thought as much of going to
Europe or North America as they did of going to the moon: life was
local. Today, these people still don't have electricity in their homes,
but the village generator powers a television that shows Hollywood
sit-coms. They may not wear shoes, but they most likely know someone who has a family member living in a big city, maybe even London, Paris, or New York. Most important, they are beginning to
realize that other people have it much better than they do and they
are beginning to ask why. The Bharatiya Janata Party of India lost the
election in 2004 with the motto "India Shining." Sure, people in the
big cities had plenty of money and lived in nice homes, but what
about the 80 percent of the population that lived in rural areas without clean water or good schools? India didn't look so shining to them
and they were not going to put up with any more promises that
would only be ignored after the election. The same thing is beginning to happen in China. Most of China's 1.2 billion people live in
the provinces, struggling to get by with a broken infrastructure and
no money to fix it. Meanwhile they hear about the building booms in
Beijing and Shanghai, about the first Chinese millionaires, about
punk rock and high fashion, and they ask how this can be in a Communist society, one that was created for the very purpose of treating
everyone equally. When most people suffer while a minority pros-
pers, trouble often follows.

I have talked about two thresholds that we are crossing: one where
the ability to cause mass destruction is spreading from the level of
the major nation-state to the level of the small country, group, or individual; and one where the speed of events is exceeding our ability

to plan a rational response. Put the two together and we face a situation where events can happen faster than we can think about them and where the consequences of those events can change history. We are rapidly approaching a future frightening enough and real enough that governments must change their priorities and the way that they think about and solve problems. It will not help to have a thousand warships or a million soldiers if the threat is a vial of bacteria carried in a terrorist's pocket. Even the most impressive array of spy satellites cannot see into the hearts and minds of people, especially when they operate in a culture that idolizes suicide as a path to paradise in the world beyond. We need to look at the fundamental causes of human violence, especially mass violence, which is emerging as the ultimate threat to our species. Rather than bullets and bombs, the most valuable weapons in the arsenal of the future will be an understanding of what motivates people to commit acts of mass violence, a realistic estimate of the factors that limit our action, and a set of concrete programs to reduce the threat of mass destruction. We will discuss each of these challenges in turn.

PART I || setting the stage:
human beings and the
societies we live in

ONE ‖ do our genes condemn us to war?

Little by little we human beings are
confronted with situations that give us
more and more clues that we aren't
perfect.

—FRED ROGERS

Dawn was still a promise on the horizon as the tugboats peeled away
for their return to port. After gently nudging the massive submarine
from the dock, the tugs shielded us from shoreline threats as we inched
down the long channel connecting the submarine base at Kings Bay,
Georgia, to the Atlantic Ocean. I had eagerly accepted an offer to ride
atop the conning tower (the "sail") of the USS *Pennsylvania* on this
one-day familiarization cruise. When we reached the open ocean, I
found it exhilarating to watch such a magnificent machine being su-
perbly handled, to feel the wind in my face, and to see the waves surge
across the partially submerged hull. There was a feeling of speed, of
power, and, quite honestly, of pride in being an American.

Later, in the control room, I was asked to sit at the diving station
and operate the controls that submerged the ship. Personally, I would
not have chosen a theoretical physicist—someone who has learned

through painful experience to keep his hands in his pockets when around anything with moving or breakable parts—to submerge a ballistic missile submarine. Nevertheless, with help from the gruff (and somewhat nervous-looking) petty officer standing behind me, the evolution was completed without incident and soon we were cruising serenely three hundred feet beneath the surface of the sea.

The Trident class of ballistic missile submarines is the most powerful weapons system on earth. Over 500 feet long and weighing in at almost 19,000 tons, it is bigger and faster than a World War I battle cruiser. It was built for the sole purpose of carrying twenty-four D5 missiles, the most accurate long-range ballistic missiles ever developed, each capable of hurling multiple nuclear warheads over distances of thousands of miles with astonishing accuracy. A modern ballistic missile submarine can stay submerged for months at a time and is so quiet that even the most advanced sonar technology cannot locate it as it creeps along a patrol path known only to its captain and senior officers.

At the time of my short voyage in 2000, I was head of nuclear weapons programs at Los Alamos and a member of the Strategic Advisory Group (SAG) at U.S. Strategic Command, the military organization that controlled all American nuclear weapons. The purpose of the cruise was to familiarize SAG members with the Trident submarine, and we enjoyed free run of the ship. Most impressive, as I always found when aboard navy ships, was the remarkable quality of the crew, both officers and enlisted, all of whom seemed truly enthusiastic about their jobs. Several of my colleagues and I chatted with the ship's nuclear reactor operators while they sat at their stations, patiently scanning dials and display screens. "Couldn't this be done automatically?" we asked. "Yes," they replied, "but in the event of damage to the ship it would take too long to regain situational awareness. We need to be able to respond instantly to keep power flowing to the engine and the other vital systems." In an environment unforgiving of mistakes, every eventuality was considered, every contingency planned. Absolute excellence was the minimum standard to be met.

Just aft of the sail was the beginning of the "missile house" with its two parallel rows of twelve rust-colored cylinders extending from the bottom to the top of the ship, each of which held a D5 missile with its several warheads. There was a wide corridor between them—almost an avenue, given the tight confines of a submarine—that gave the missile house the appearance of a metallic forest. I have been in these rooms a number of times, always with the realization that I was in the presence of incredible power, something unique in human experience. There was a presence in that room full of missiles, a kind of hush in which the theory of mutually assured destruction became very, very real.

Popular movies on nuclear war, from *Fail Safe* to *Crimson Tide*, portray the moral dilemma that a commanding officer might undergo if he or she received orders to actually launch a nuclear holocaust. "Yes, New York, Washington, and Los Angeles are gone, but is that worth taking hundreds of thousands of other lives, essentially in revenge? Where does it stop?" Close-up and fade to credits. I don't think so. Having watched numerous exercises that simulated multiple launches of nuclear missiles, there is no doubt in my mind that, should the president of the United States so order, missile after missile would leave its silo with clockwork precision. The Emergency Action Message (EAM) would be received. Safes would be opened to extract sealed validation codes. The codes would be checked, checked again, and checked yet again. If it was a match, a rapid sequence of well-practiced actions would commence, each one accompanied by a loud but controlled confirmation of its completion. When the lights were all green, the launch control officer would press the trigger on his handheld controller, there would be a gentle thud, and a crewman would report "Missile away." Within seconds, they would move on to the next launch. Within minutes, an explosive force greater than all the weapons used in all the wars in history would be flying toward its intended target. After that there would be time for the crew members to think, time to come to terms with what they had done, and time to pray.

It is not that these sailors and airmen lack moral feeling or that they are somehow more bloodthirsty than the rest of us. Yes, they are trained in the most destructive military science. Yet they are ordinary people, with families and careers, law-abiding and gentle with children; many are deeply religious and all are intensely patriotic. And it's not only violence-prone males who do such work; women also do silo duty and perform with the same dedication and precision. Whatever reservations they have about their jobs have long since been thought through. They have no desire to kill other people, but they do believe that a country perceived to be weak on defense is inviting an attack on itself. Their job is to assure all comers that any aggression against the United States would have fatal consequences for the aggressor.

As much as one feels a presence in the missile house of the *Pennsylvania*, there is an even stronger presence felt on another ship, the USS *Arizona*, resting on the bottom of Pearl Harbor where it was bombed and blew up on December 7, 1941. More than a historical landmark, the *Arizona* is a tomb for over one thousand sailors who never escaped the explosions and fire that marked the death throes of a symbol of American naval power. An awesome quiet reigns on the white concrete memorial that spans the remains of the ship, a quiet that leaves each person to his or her thoughts about what can happen when a country is unprepared. Some remember the boyish faces of crewmates who were last seen on a warm Hawaiian Saturday night.

Others stare at the names inscribed in marble of never-seen fathers or grandfathers; in front of a memorial wall dozens of flowered leis rest atop what looks like an altar railing.

Once, on an official visit to Pacific Command, our small group had the opportunity to be alone with the *Arizona*, the only sounds those of the lapping waves and the flags ruffling overhead. Drops of oil, still leaking from the wreck, rose slowly to the surface to spread in a beautiful rainbow pattern, a pattern in which one was tempted to read "Don't forget... don't forget... don't forget..."

Most of us will never have to face the responsibility of launching a nuclear attack against another country or defending our own country against a surprise attack, but that does not absolve us of the responsibility of thinking about how we should behave in a manifestly dangerous world. Would you feel safer if your country gave up its nuclear weapons, trusting in the reciprocal goodness of your fellow human beings? Would we be better off disarming completely, ensuring that mass destruction was no longer possible? "What if they gave a war and nobody came?" asked the old antiwar slogan. Before you answer, it is worth reviewing some facts about our species, the most complex species ever to walk the earth, a species capable of the most heartwarming generosity and the most heartrending brutality, a violent species prone to playing with fire.

Each year about 17,000 people in the United States are murdered, most by people well known to them. That's a rate of 5.6 murders per 100,000 people in the population, a standard measure used by the world's law enforcement community. The American homicide rate is considerably higher than other countries such as England and Wales

(1.6) and Switzerland (0.96), but it is lower than Russia with its value of 21.4 murders per 100,000 people. Homicide has occurred in every culture in every period. No group seems immune to murder or the temptation to commit it.

Different cultures have very different attitudes toward violence. In Afghanistan it was, until quite recently, not a crime to kill someone if it was done in a fair fight. Indeed, in that warrior culture, for a male to reach the age of maturity without having fought someone raised serious questions about his character: What type of man would not prove his bravery? The dagger presented to a boy at age 5 was not for decorative or ceremonial purposes; it was an important tool for survival in a society in which personal slights could lead to lethal bloodshed.

By way of contrast, consider the report of anthropologist Robert Borofsky regarding a potentially violent encounter that he witnessed on the tiny Pacific island of Pukapuka. Two men, one of whom felt wronged by the other, met in a jungle clearing. Immediately the injured party drew a machete and began shouting at the other man, threatening all manner of mayhem, including death. It seemed fortunate to Borofsky that two other men were nearby. They grabbed the would-be attacker by each arm and held him back from what was sure to be hot-blooded murder. Even with this restraint, the shouting and threats continued until, when the four men became tired, a break was called. Everyone stood still and things quieted down for a few moments, after which time the attacker raised his arms, allowed his two attendants to once again grab hold of them, and resumed his "attack." There was never any intention to do bodily harm, but it was important for the aggrieved party to make the impression that he was justifiably angry. He knew that actually committing a violent act would be more than frowned upon by his peers and that he could be ostracized for the offense, a fate worse than death on an isolated island in which close social interaction was the essence of life.

Most modern societies have attitudes toward violence somewhere in between the extremes of warrior Afghanistan and pacific Pukapuka. While we fret over the crime rate, most of us feel relatively safe going shopping, visiting friends, and even traveling to other cities or countries. We have developed street smarts that warn us of impending danger; we are savvy enough to avoid walking alone at night in bad neighborhoods. More than that, violence against persons is *against the law* in every civilized country. Only in cases of self-defense, and then only when the threat to our life or the life of someone nearby is imminent, is it permitted to physically injure another person, and even then there is likely to be a formal investigation to ensure that there was just cause. Governments have become the sole arbiters of when violence is justified either at an individual level in criminal proceedings or at the group level in war or genocide. Whatever your feelings about the role of "big government" in your life, it is a fact that increased governmental oversight of society has been accompanied by a corresponding reduction in the amount of civil violence. Murder rates in Western nations are much lower today then they were a century ago. Going further back, archeological data indicate that in some hunter-gatherer societies deaths due to homicide and war comprised an astonishing 40 to 60 percent of adult mortality.

However, look at the other side of the story: violence in warfare or genocide that is perpetrated by groups of people operating with the official sponsorship of their government. Here the picture is much less rosy, as can be seen by even the most cursory examination of the history of the twentieth century. Although accurate statistics are hard to come by, the total number of civil homicides from 1900 to 1999 was a little less than 10 million. In contrast, the number of government-sponsored deaths—war and genocide—is estimated at over 100 million. Despite our high level of civilization, we have repeatedly gone to war and killed millions in the process. War has progressed from the confrontation of professional armies to include the systematic extermination of millions of innocent civilians, people whose only "crime" was to have a different religious or ethnic background than the majority. Most who committed those heinous acts were civilized people not so very different from you or me. What caused them to do these things? Why do we suspend our normal behavior, take up guns, and kill people whom we have never met, people with whom we have no personal quarrel, people who have families, hopes, and aspirations very similar to our own? Here are two particularly illustrative examples of our willingness to kill and be killed that evoke the madness of mass violence. Both are from World War I, a conflict sufficiently distant from us that we can think about it objectively, yet close enough that we can relate to the individuals and societies involved.

July 1, 1916, was the first day of the battle of the Somme, one of the largest and bloodiest battles of what was then called the Great War. For almost two years, British and German troops had faced one another across fixed trench lines, a stalemate that appeared to have no end, one that was steadily sapping the morale and resources of both sides. Something had to be done to break the deadlock and, in an act motivated by equal doses of boldness and frustration, the British general staff decided to act. All through the night of June 30, British artillery pounded German positions with tens of thousands of high explosive shells, hoping to create a gap in the lines through which infantry could advance the following morning. Just after dawn, at a precisely appointed time, officers blew whistles and thousands of Tommys rose from their trenches. Far from a mad dash across no-man's-land, they calmly walked abreast in line formation, always remaining within shouting distance of their sergeants and captains, seemingly oblivious of the carnage that German machine guns were causing around them. (During the artillery barrage the Germans retreated to deep bunkers, only to reemerge when the British commenced their attack.) Wave after wave of British soldiers advanced and wave after wave was mowed down like stalks of wheat before the scythe. By the end of the day, over 60,000 British soldiers had been killed or wounded. Was this enough to convince their commanders that marching slowly toward machine guns was not a good idea? Unfortunately not, for the next day the battle resumed with the same tactics and the same results. This continued the next day and the day after that, well into the month of July.

Now change sides and consider the epic battle between the French and Germans at Verdun. For years, the French had worked on a line of fortresses a few hours' drive north of Paris. They were considered impregnable icons of French military engineering, and hence positions to be held at all cost. The Germans knew this and decided that Verdun was the perfect place to "bleed the French army white." They launched titanic artillery barrages against French soldiers hunkered down in and about their concrete pillboxes. In some areas, over a thousand shells fell *per square yard* of the battlefield. After a barrage, German soldiers who only months before had been at school reading the classics advanced on machine guns manned by French soldiers who had been reading the same classics in their own schools. By the end of the battle, nearly 1 *million* men had been killed, wounded, or gone missing—with no change in the position of the front line. I visited Verdun one cold morning and was surprised to see the area around the forts still a sea of frozen brown waves left from the explosions of millions of artillery shells. After almost a century, the earth had yet to heal.

You might think that you would never agree to walk bolt upright into machine gun fire, knowing full well that you would likely be killed. Nor would you ever sit behind one of those machine guns and callously slaughter your fellow human beings. Nothing could ever make you do those things, right? Maybe you would have been one of the very small number of soldiers who claimed status as conscientious objectors, but much more likely you would have taken your place if called upon, and done so with enthusiasm. The people who fought in these battles were not brutes or people who had no regard for life or property. Many of the British officers who stepped out of the trenches on July 1, 1916, were brilliant and sensitive men; some were poets, others composers, some were members of the privileged aristocracy; almost all of them had been willing volunteers. The German soldiers who killed them came from the best-educated nation of Europe, a place of great authors and scientists, a country that was considered a paragon of civilization and culture. What caused ordinary people, even extraordinary people, to kill one another, seemingly with so little reluctance?

Put yourself in their place for a moment to see how you too could become ready to kill and be killed. Consider yourself a young British man at university, quietly pursuing a career with no interest in international affairs beyond where you might take a pleasant holiday. You have read for years about the growing threat of the German army and navy, the vast sums that Germany was spending on new armaments. Clearly this is a challenge to the British Empire, the greatest force for good in the history of the world, which has lifted hundreds of millions of unfortunate people out of barbarism and onto the path to civilization. The German attack on Belgium and France in August 1914 only confirms your suspicions about the aggressive Hun, and you read about how hundreds of thousands of loyal Britons are rallying to defend "little Belgium." With increasing social pressure, or perhaps out of a newfound sense of patriotism, you volunteer and are sent to training camp. Here your world is turned upside down. Your military instructors begin to systematically demolish your value system and replace it with one based on loyalty to comrades and obedience to orders, relentlessly training you to put others above self. Mindless exercises drill into you the need to obey orders without thinking: on the battlefield events happen too quickly for each person to decide his own course of action. A new reward system replaces the one that you left behind, a reward system based on heroism and derring-do, on the mystique and glory of battle and those who bravely sacrifice themselves for their comrades. You go to France with men who have become as close to you as any family member or friend. The whistle blows and you do what you have been trained to do.

The willingness to be a part of war is not limited to soldiers. In 1943, a group of the best scientists in the world met at a ranch school in Los Alamos, New Mexico, to plan the construction of the first atomic bomb. Leading the team was J. Robert Oppenheimer, a shy but determined university professor who had made his name in the heady world of quantum theory. He was a former socialist and about the last person you might expect to oversee one of the largest and most secret weapons programs in history.

Oppenheimer gathered around him the greatest concentration of physics talent in history. Hans Bethe, who discovered what causes the stars to burn and who would remain connected to the nuclear weapons program for decades as both critic and conscience, led the theoretical effort. John von Neumann, a mathematician who invented entire areas of what would later become computer science, oversaw some of the mammoth calculations that were required to design the first "gadget." Edward Teller, an impatient Hungarian émigré, looked beyond the next horizon and argued passionately for the development of the hydrogen bomb, an even more powerful explosive that appeared to have no limit on its destructive potential.

The team worked with a zeal that came from believing that the best way to aid the war effort was to create a device that would end it. Few of the geniuses toiling on the New Mexico mesas would have made good soldiers, but all of them were terrified of what would happen if Germany got the bomb first. Many had studied in Germany and some had fled the Gestapo with little more than the clothes on their backs.

When the world's first nuclear detonation occurred in the flat desert at Alamogordo—an event that, despite all the calculations and estimates of its power, shocked the scientists who were gathered to watch—Oppenheimer thought of the ancient Hindu scripture, "Now I am become Death, the destroyer of Worlds." He knew that it was he, more than anyone else, who had unleashed this incredible force upon the world. After the test, arguments about the first "tactical" use of the bomb intensified, with some senior scientists insisting that the Japanese should be invited to a demonstration in the hope that it would convince them of the futility of continuing to fight. In the end, it was President Truman who made the decision to drop the bombs on Hiroshima and Nagasaki, but the scientists felt responsible for creating the weapon.

After the war, Oppenheimer argued against further work on nuclear weapons or, at the very least, for international controls. But the very arms race he sought to stop was a driving force for Edward Teller, whose passion to create a superbomb only grew with time. Teller went so far as to cast doubt on Oppenheimer's loyalty, and eventually the government revoked Oppenheimer's security clearances, a stinging insult to someone who had given so much to his country. In 1989, I moved from Livermore, where I had done nuclear weapons design, to Los Alamos, in the hope of pursuing research in plasma physics. I was surprised that, even after more than forty years, there remained a strong feeling against Teller, a belief that he had smeared a good and noble man who had only tried to do what he thought was right.

Oppenheimer's spirit lives on at Los Alamos. When I interviewed people for jobs I would quickly check their résumés for the required stellar grades in physics, engineering, or mathematics. This told me how quickly they could pick up new concepts and use them to solve problems. I would then see how many papers they had published, as an indicator of how productive they were. But if I was really interested in someone I would look for their credentials and interests beyond science and technology. Had they taken much history, any philosophy, any other social sciences or humanities in college? I wanted more than a technician—someone who knew *how* to do science. Our work affected the future of the world and I wanted people who understood *why* they were doing it. I sought out candidates who could put their work into a historical perspective and, if the occasion arose, have the gumption to say no.

Sometimes mass violence involves perfectly ordinary civilians who had, only weeks before, lived in peaceful harmony with their neighbors. In 1984, the government of Rwanda went on the radio to encourage the Hutu majority to kill as many of their Tutsi neighbors as they could. No advanced technology was required since machetes, axes, and kitchen knives would get the job done. To encourage those who might have second thoughts, the government proclaimed that anyone caught slacking in his or her quota of deaths would themselves be killed. Over 800,000 people perished in the slaughter, many of them children. You might dismiss this as tribal warfare, a remnant of a savage past. If you are especially empathetic, you express horror and outrage, demanding that something be done. If you had only known, you surely would have stepped in to prevent such a tragedy. Well, the fact is that we did know—we intercepted the radio broadcasts and we watched the butchery on the evening news.

Committing violence is one thing; standing by and letting it happen is another. And our indifference is not limited to violence committed on the other side of the world. Consider the case of Kitty Genovese, a woman who was attacked in the spring of 1964 outside a New York apartment house while dozens of people looked down from their windows. No one came to her aid and no one bothered to call the police. "I didn't want to get involved," was the typical excuse. When the Jews were pulled from their homes in Nazi Germany, it was manifestly obvious to the German population that innocent people were being brutalized. We knew that the Rwandan government was actively inciting genocide, we knew that the Serbian government was actively promoting "ethnic cleansing," and we knew that the Sudanese government was at least allowing (if not actively promoting) genocide in Darfur. Only in the case of Serbia was there any response, and then only after the situation had gone well beyond irreparable damage.

Why? Cynics point out that in both African countries the victims were black, different from the rich white populations of the developed world. They also argue that if there was more oil in those places, the world would have quickly intervened, as it indeed did after the Iraqi invasion of Kuwait.

Racism and economics might explain some instances of inaction in the face of genocide, but not all of them. The Jews in Germany were no different from their neighbors; their only crime was being Jewish. There was incredible talent in the Jewish community, much of which was lost in the Holocaust. Wouldn't Germany have been better off keeping Einstein and many other brilliant scientists than driving them away or killing them?

There is another even more cynical explanation for our complacency when the victim's suffering has no bearing on our own life and happiness. Sudanese refugees are far away, and no matter what happens to them, it is unlikely that it will affect our quality of life as Americans. There is a cost to doing something—and no cost for doing nothing. Maybe we would feel better if we helped, but the feelgood factor is seldom enough to goad people into action, even when suffering is headline news every day.

Maybe you wouldn't walk into an advancing artillery barrage with your chums, volunteer to create a bomb of unprecedented power, or be a participant in genocide. Maybe you really *are* peaceful, meaning no one any harm, the very model of a modern civilized person. But how long has it been since you paid to see someone killed in a movie and then walked out of the theater saying, "That was a good movie!"? How long has it been since you cheered as your favorite football player brutally tackled a player on the opposing team? Have you read any good thrillers lately? Violence is a staple of our entertainment industry; regularly bringing in millions of dollars per movie, bestselling book, or video game. As retired air force general Larry Welch wryly observed, "Anyone who thinks that the United States doesn't have the stomach for a fight doesn't know that we spend seventeen billion dollars a year on professional football." How many children in your neighborhood will spend Christmas morning killing mutants on Planet Zylon and exulting in the points they score? The jury is still out on the impact of violent entertainment on individual development, but I think it safe to say that watching gratuitous violence is hardly an inducement to pacifism.

What is the root cause of human violence, of our willingness to haphazardly or systematically kill one another? Is it in our genes, a holdover from our distant hunter ancestors who killed for food, for mates, and to defend their families? Or is it something learned, something that we could eliminate if we could only find the ideal social system or the perfect way to educate our young people? Passionate advocates exist on both sides of this issue. Since murder occurs in every socioeconomic stratum, there is some justification for concluding that we have a violent streak in our nature. Given the right circumstances, almost anyone is capable of killing. It is also true that the rates of violence are much higher in some communities than they are in others. There is a strong positive correlation between individuals who are raised in a violent environment and the probability that they will themselves commit a violent act at some point in their lives.

As with many things, the truth about the origin of violence lies somewhere between nature and nurture. There is most certainly a genetic (or biological) component to human violence, but it also seems likely that frequent exposure to violence induces a person to consider it a viable means for resolving disputes, for getting a point across, or just to relieve frustration. The good news about the nature argument is that the murder rate is relatively low for the total population—very few people actually try to kill someone. The good news about the nurture argument is that it may be possible to change the conditions that result in learned violence, not an easy thing to be sure, but one that is at least possible.

Most homicides are crimes of passion, but warfare and genocide are premeditated actions on the part of a government with the willing support of the population. There is a large literature on the causes of war, but it is sufficient to say that the old motivations of greed, fear, and revenge loom large as reasons for one group to attack another. Prior to World War I, Germany wanted more access to lucrative colonial trade. Prior to World War II, Japan wanted access to natural resources vital to its expanding industrial economy. In 2003, the United States was afraid of Saddam Hussein getting weapons of mass destruction. And the list goes on. What differentiates homicide from warfare is that the former involves one or a few individuals who most often know one another, frequently acting in a fit of anger. Warfare involves carefully calculated clashes of thousands who are complete strangers. It is unrealistic, knowing what we do about human beings, that we could stop every crime of passion. But we should be able to do something about organized violence—genocide and warfare—which took far more lives in the twentieth century than did simple murder.

During most of our history, we could segregate human violence into the two categories: individual homicide and organized warfare between nations. Today we face a third type: organized international terrorism. Neither a spontaneous crime of passion nor an act of state-sponsored war, it shares some of the characteristics of both. Terrorists are driven by hatred and believe that their objectives can only be reached by violence, so in this sense passion motivates their actions. However, most terrorists neither know nor care to know their victims and they plot their actions with ruthless premeditation. In this sense, terrorism is like warfare. The proliferation of weapons of mass destruction blurs the distinction between terrorism and warfare even further. Today we face terrorists who can kill thousands with truck bombs and hijacked airplanes. In the future, we will face terrorists armed with chemical, biological, or even nuclear weapons—weapons that can kill hundreds of thousands or even millions at a time. It will be the worst of all possible situations—a group driven by passion with the ability to inflict mass casualties. Whereas in the past we could apply one set of solutions to individual violence and another to international violence, in the future we will need to address the root causes of *all* violence.

It is not just that we humans are potentially violent, awaiting only the right situation to trigger an innate capability. There are other human attributes that complicate our understanding of violence. Human beings are *social animals* who need to be part of a group. Without social companionship, otherwise healthy infants will die and adults will lose their reason. And family is not enough. So strong is our need for companionship that we create artificial organizations such as fan clubs and political groups for the sole purpose of being around other people who have similar interests. Once we join the club or get the bumper sticker, we cede part of our identity to that group. We *are* a Republican or a Rotarian or a Yankees fan. From there, it's only a hop, skip, and jump to distancing ourselves from people who are Democrats, Lions, or Dodgers fans.

A counterpart to our need for companionship is our ability to label and alienate people. When we put a label on a person, then that person becomes the label rather than a real human being with whom we might empathize. And once that happens, it is easier for us to do things to that person, or allow things to be done, that we would never permit if we thought of him or her in the same way as we do a family member. In essence, alienation allows us to dehumanize people and feel less remorse about what happens to them.

A second complication is that we are by nature *competitive animals*. Few of us compete for food anymore, and most of us can find a mate, so the original motivations for competition are lost in mists of time. However, the urge to do better than other people continues to be a potent driver of human action. There is social status to be gained from competition and a concomitant sense of self-worth. If there is no real *need* to compete, we will create one. How much do we spend on clothes, luxury cars, or homes? Some business leaders work to beat the competition long after they have accumulated more money than they will ever spend. Most of us actually enjoy competition for its own sake; we like to win.

So our challenge in dealing with large-scale violence, the major cause of death in the twentieth century and the greatest threat that we face in the future, comes down to three fundamental aspects of our own humanity. First, while we may not be inherently violent as individuals, we have the *potential* for violence if we are placed in the right circumstances. Second, our need for companionship drives us to belong to groups, from families to nations, with the associated ability to alienate and dehumanize those in other groups. Third, we are naturally competitive and like to show our superiority, including through the use of violence.

It is doubtful at best that we could change any of these basic human traits, or at least change them soon enough to avoid an impending catastrophe involving weapons of mass destruction. However, recognizing the causes of a problem is the first step toward its solution. Being alert to the warning signals of unbridled international competition, being sensitive to the results of victory on the battlefield or in the marketplace, and understanding that the power of future weaponry makes *any* war a threat to *all* people, could and should cause us to take a fresh look at how we manage our affairs. We are potentially violent, we are social animals, and we are competitive, but these factors alone do not in and of themselves condemn us to a future of mass destruction.

History shows again and again that good wishes alone are not enough to prevent bad things from happening. Hope is not a plan. Rather than searching for *perfect* worlds, let us consider how we might construct the best *practical* world consistent with our human nature. Let us look for ways to eliminate the large-scale violence that we can see coming, violence that requires detailed planning and buy-in from large numbers of people. While crimes of passion may be impossible to eliminate totally, we may be able to reduce the likelihood of serious international confrontations. Given the aggressive character of some national leaders, we *may* not be able to eliminate all warfare. However, we might reduce the probability of the kind of large-scale warfare that took tens of millions of lives in the last century. There may be no way to prevent an individual terrorist from committing an isolated bombing, but we may be able to reduce the number of recruits to his cause, making him much less capable of planning and executing acts of mass destruction.

But before we begin tinkering with the world's social and political systems, let's look at how they got to be that way. There may be reasons why things are the way they are.

some useful lessons from history

*I am afraid that man today is merely an
extension of what man always was, only
more complicated.* —VITA SACKVILLE-WEST

Steve Tinney is a very contented person. As associate curator of the
Babylonian collection of the University of Pennsylvania Museum of
Archeology and Anthropology, he oversees one of the largest collections of the oldest documents anywhere in the world. It is an arcane
field to say the least—only a few hundred people can read Sumerian,
the language in which many of the inscriptions were written, and
very few of those have daily access to a collection as magnificent
as the one at Penn. "We actually discourage people from going into
the field," he told me. "We tell them, 'There are no jobs today, there
never *were* any jobs, and there never *will be* any jobs. Only do this
if you can't think of being happy doing anything else.' " Steve is one
of those people who cannot imagine doing anything but what he
is doing.

He is remarkably patient with the enthusiastic amateur in his
office. We quickly move beyond what he calls the "dessert cart" of
artifacts usually shown to visiting VIPs and into the meat of the

collection. "Do you have the inscription where a father gives advice to his son?" I ask. A bit of computer detective work indicated that he does, and in a moment it is in my hand, a tablet that is over 4,000 years old, more remote to the Romans than the Romans are to us. Only a fragment of the original and hardly bigger than a cell phone, it is covered with a mass of what look like hen pecks but which are actually cuneiform signs impressed upon once-wet clay. I find it curious that this tablet, which I have read many times in translation, is "dead"—devoid of any of the magic that one might expect from so ancient an object. "I feel the same way," Dr. Tinney told me. "Maybe it's just that they are so old—all the life has gone out of them. The scribes that wrote them are just too remote. A colleague once asked me if I could hear the scratching of the scribe's stylus as I read the tablet. I said, 'No, that's just the air conditioning.' "

But while the tablets themselves may be dead, the inscriptions that cover them are as fresh and alive as the day that they were written. Here we can read of the invention of government, the development of religions, and, on a more mundane level, love poems, business receipts, and even homesick letters to mothers. The Sumerians wrote on clay, and once it hardened, it was almost impervious to the vicissitudes of history. Clay only gets harder, surviving fires and 5,000 years of being buried in the sand. If the world were to end today in a nuclear firestorm, one of the largest surviving collections of human documents would be written in cuneiform on clay dug up from the banks of the Tigris and Euphrates Rivers thousands of years ago.

I was at the University Museum in Philadelphia to give a public lecture on how the Sumerians shaped Western civilization. For thirty years I have been fascinated with the Sumerians and their legacy to Greece, Rome, Europe, and ultimately the United States. When I was in graduate school, I taught myself Sumerian cuneiform just for the pleasure of being able to read the oldest written documents in their original form. I wanted to get closer to the people who had such an influence on Western culture. When the slate of human civilization was nearly blank, why did people choose to do things the way they did, and not some other way? From their texts, art work, cities, and monumental architecture, we can see that the Sumerians had a complex, highly developed culture.

Before we think about changing the social and political systems that seem to be the cause of mass violence, it might be a good idea to understand how and why those institutions came about in the first place. And to do that we might as well go back to the very beginning.

Anthropologists make a convincing case that the earliest human beings lived in groups of a few dozen without much in the way of formal leadership. With so few people, most of them part of an extended family, decisions could be made by consensus, hashed out around the campfire or while searching for food. Within an extended family, issues of ownership and fairness could be resolved through informal discussion. But when population density increased and whole groups came into conflict with one another, informal discussion was no longer practical or possible. To simplify things, a "big man" was appointed to shepherd the group through difficult times and to represent the group in negotiations with other groups. The position was intended to be temporary but, human nature being what it is, the difficult times became frequent enough to require a full-time leader. (One can also imagine that the big man grew to enjoy his authority and thought that it would be nice to have it all the time.) But this leads to a delicate problem: If a permanent leader is needed, how should that leader be chosen and how should challenges to his leadership be handled? Having constant fights about who would be the big man would be worse than having no leader at all.

We have the actual text in which the Sumerians solved this problem, perhaps the most profound political statement ever written: "When kingship descended from heaven." These words begin the Sumerian king list, which, as the name implies, is a list of the kings of Sumerian cities along with the lengths of their reigns. The opening line is stunning in its simplicity and its implications for history: "When" suggests there was a time when kingship did not exist; "kingship" embodies the idea of one above all others; and "descended from heaven" carries the notion that the king received his mandate directly from the gods. In just a few cuneiform signs the concept of divine right of kings was invented, a system of government that dominated Western civilization right up into the twentieth century.

Interesting perhaps, but how is this ancient history relevant to the problem of mass violence in the modern world, one that is dominated by technologies undreamed of by the Sumerians? Here's how. Genetic evidence supports the notion that human beings have changed little over the past 5,000 years, the span of recorded history. We have better tools and we have much more experience in dealing with the world and one another, but as humans we aren't much different from the "black-headed people" (as the Sumerians called themselves) who invented so many elements of our culture and left the records to prove it. The Sumerians were faced with the same generic types of problems that we face today—how to organize and govern large numbers of people and how to interact with other groups in an efficient manner. What is so significant about the notion of divine right of kings, a system that few people today would like to see return, is that it was an *invented thing*. While we don't get to choose how tall we are or how many fingers we have, we did and do choose how we organize ourselves.

Central governments do not appear to be the result of any innate human need to be under a leader. Many indigenous peoples around the world lived and continue to live quite nicely in egalitarian societies, ones without any hierarchical leadership, where decisions affecting the group are made by consensus. However, this is not because such people are somehow more peaceful than the rest of us, or less ambitious and more willing to accept the status quo. Anthropologist Christopher Boehm makes the point that they have to *work at it* to keep upstarts from assuming leadership and possibly pushing the population into expansion and warfare. Through a relentless process of ridicule, self-depreciation, and sometimes even murder, they actively suppress individual leaders in what Boehm calls "reverse-dominance hierarchy." In effect, egalitarian peoples *invented* their own system of social control, one that prevented individuals from coming to prominence. While most societies made the transition to some form of central government, some didn't—an indication that we are not biologically bound to any particular form of governance.

A clue to why most societies made the shift to central government lies in the fact that most egalitarian cultures consist of groups of a few hundred people or less, groups that live in relative isolation from one another. Nowhere do we know of a completely egalitarian society consisting of many thousands of persons. As population density increases, as the demands for the organized division of labor become greater, societies find that they needed to concentrate decision making. But why choose monarchy, a system that led to near-constant conflict among the Sumerian city-states and in just about every civilization in which it was tried? While one shouldn't second-guess over a distance of five millennia, I think it is reasonable to posit that it was because the alternatives simply didn't work. Apparently, the Sumerians started as an egalitarian society or at least one ruled by a council of elders. The fact that they went through the big man stage of government is indicated by the fact that the Sumerian word for king was *lu-gal*, literally "man-big." The options were chaos or strong central government, and the Sumerians chose strong central government with a bulletproof justification to preclude all but the most determined challenges to its legitimacy.

None of this should be too surprising. Families sit around the kitchen table and work out disputes, coming to agreement or compromising on difficult points. We can use the same egalitarian method when two or three families get together to plan a cookout or talk about fencing backyards. But when fifty families need to interact with fifty other families, things can get pretty complicated. In those cases we permit one or more people to represent us, trusting them to negotiate on behalf of everyone, essentially giving up some of our own authority in the interest of efficiency and the common good. But how do we make sure that the leader represents our interests and not his or her own? The problem with absolute monarchies, especially those based on inheritance of title, was that one could never be sure that the leader would have the welfare of the people at heart. Some kings were true leaders, visionaries who carried their country to the next level. Others were incompetent or, even worse, tyrants who extorted money from the people and led them to ruinous wars.

The solution to the problem of choosing a suitable leader for a large population was democracy—a fundamental shift in the justification of authority. Compare the words of the Sumerian king list to the opening words of the Constitution of the United States, which begins, "We the people." No longer was a leader given absolute power in the *hope* that he would use that power to the benefit of the people. In the new scheme, the *people themselves* chose their leader and provided the ultimate justification for his or her authority. This last point was essential to avoiding a drift back to absolute power. What if, once in office, a leader changed his stripes and started to abuse his position? Being able to remove a leader through a regularly scheduled election is as important as the power to install the leader in the first place.

Other countries experimented with elected leadership before the United States. Greece and Rome had forms of democracy, albeit with a very limited franchise, but they both slipped back to absolute rule. England attempted to combine the benefits of centralized power with democracy by creating a constitutional monarchy with an elected parliament to provide a balance against the power of the king. However, in most of these cases there were still few checks on the power of the government once it was in place. Rulers and parliaments could be elected and they could sometimes be removed, but it was difficult to constrain them while they were in office.

The founders of the United States struggled to create a management system that avoided the problems encountered by past democracies. Recognizing the dangers of too much power in too few hands, they purposefully divided power not just between a ruler and a parliament, but between *three* components: the administrative, legislative, and judiciary branches. The administration was designed to run the country, to provide the type of central leadership that is effective at getting things done. The legislative branch, itself divided into two parts, was given the power to make the laws that governed both the people and the administration. One of the problems with previous implementations of democracy was that, once in power, the government could change the laws to suit its own purposes. The American system avoids this temptation by separating the making of laws from their implementation. And to prevent a paralyzing war of wills between two power centers, an umpire was created in the form of an independent judiciary that could resolve disagreements short of dissolving the government. Finally, our government is based upon the assumption that everyone, regardless of position, is subject to the rule of law and that the ultimate authority in the nation is the will of the people as voiced in periodic elections. While not perfect, the American system of government was a brilliant invention that has survived two centuries of testing. It has enabled us to become one of the most successful cultures of all time.

There are two points to draw from this discussion: First, the political and social systems in which we live are not inevitable; they are not the only way that human beings can organize themselves. They are *invented things*. While large populations require structure to operate efficiently, nothing mandates what *type* of structure we create. Second, as invented things *social systems can be changed*. The Sumerians gave up rule by council and invested power in a single leader, legitimizing him by invoking divine mandate. Societies throughout history have oscillated between democracy and absolute government, trading the efficiency of strong leadership for the benefits of limiting the abuse of power, then moving back to strong central government when factional arguments in the bureaucracy failed to deliver on expectations. And it wasn't just because someone came along who was stronger and imposed his rule upon an unwilling population. Monarchies and other forms of absolute governments arose to solve problems, even if they created an even bigger set along the way. Lenin and Hitler each arose from the democratic chaos surrounding the collapse of monarchy—in neither Russia nor Germany could representative governments take hold and form a workable social system. Lots of people *voted* for Hitler. Stalin, who killed more Russians than Hitler, is still considered a good leader by many Russians. The form of government that seems to work best is a democracy where the people are given the opportunity to choose their leaders and where the government is divided into parts to provide for internal checks and balances on the exercise of power.

Democracy does more than prevent the abuse of power. The ability to change government and chart a new course satisfies another fundamental human requirement—our need to constantly reinvent ourselves, to explore new frontiers. Human society is fundamentally *dynamic*: we seem unable to remain in a stable equilibrium for very long. Empires and civilizations either expand or contract, wax or wane, but they never stay the same for any length of time. The Sumerians bickered among themselves and were conquered by the Babylonians. Alexander the Great conquered the Babylonians and the rest of the known world of his time, weeping when there were no more lands of value to add to his empire. But had he lived, could even Alexander have kept his empire together after the conquest phase was over? Could he have dealt with feeding the people, keeping commerce flowing, suppressing upstarts, and so on? The Romans built a magnificent civilization, but it collapsed under its own weight as greedy citizens fought and bought their way to imperial privilege. Napoleon captured the energy of a people who had fought a revolution against a repressive monarchy, only to have his own empire collapse under the combined pressure of the other European powers. Twice in the twentieth century Germany tried to expand its reach, and twice it was beaten back. In all of the 5,000 years of history that begins with Steve Tinney's clay tablets there are few, if any, cases of a single social or political entity enduring for more than a few centuries. China and Japan, so proud of the antiquity of their imperial families, each had many periods of internal discord when the emperor's power was disputed or was little more than symbolic. Situations change, people die, and new people come along to replace them, each bringing their own drive to excel, to create, and sometimes to rule. New technologies appear—iron ships and airplanes and rockets that, combined with the uneven distribution of natural resources around the world, give one group an advantage over another. Even the lack of any external enemy does not insure stability. Rome conquered most everything worth conquering. Its downfall was not so much a result of barbarian invasion as of internal rot that allowed the barbarians through the gate. If seems that if we lack an external enemy, someone or something to challenge us to do better, we will relax and decay.

Think about this in your own life. Have you ever reached the limits of a job and become restless and unhappy, aware that you could do more, anxious for new challenges? Your job may have satisfied all your basic needs, but it was somehow not *satisfying*, you wanted *more*. We are a restless species, one that is constantly looking toward the horizon, seeking some new hill to climb. When someone else already occupies that hill, we are, as often as not, willing to contest ownership and fight for the prize, sometimes by our wits and sometimes with our fists. Even if you don't buy the notion that everyone is competitive, *enough* people are to make competition a significant force in human affairs. What is true for us as individuals seems also to be true when we are in groups, even groups as large as nations.

Prior to the twentieth century, wealth was measured largely in terms of land and people. Countries with a lot of land and the people to work it did well, and countries that lacked workers and resources struggled. Wars were fought to get territory, to control a larger population, and to get needed resources. And it wasn't just the expansion of the homeland. Brutal conflicts were fought to control distant colonies that served as sources of raw materials and captive markets for manufactured goods.

When the industrial revolution got into full swing in the nineteenth century, an opportunity for expansion appeared in a different dimension—industrial output. Empires were created by capturing markets rather than land, by building huge corporations that, as in the case of the British East India Company and the Standard Oil Company, vied with nation-states in the wealth that they controlled.

The United States is the most vivid and successful example of a large human organization that has managed to keep its competitive spirit going while largely avoiding the temptation of mass violence. We started with the same ideas about territory and power as most other nation-states, a policy codified in the doctrine of Manifest Destiny that sought to settle all of the lands between the Atlantic and Pacific. This accomplished, we had a brief flirtation with international imperialism, a phase marked by the Spanish-American War, but we quickly found foreign adventures ill-suited to our national character. From the beginning of the twentieth century, the United States largely refrained from the type of territorial expansion that typified empires and turned its attention to industrial production. By World War I, we were one of the dominant industrial nations of the world, and by the end of World War II the United States had the world's largest intact industrial complex. As other countries developed, and as Europe and Japan rebuilt after the war, we faced stiff competition. There was even a time when some thought that Japan would overtake us as the economic superpower, that the United States' day was over.

However, just when we seemed to reach the limits of our industrial expansion, a new domain was discovered—information technology and services—that enabled us to expand into yet another dimension. New industries based on the computer arose to challenge the most ambitious personalities and, rather than complain about what other countries were doing, we focused our energies on our own creative pursuits. No shots were fired, no territory was occupied, but once again the United States found a channel for the enthusiasm and restlessness of its people. This may be the most encouraging sign for a peaceful future. Whether there is another lily pad out there for us to jump to, one that will provide yet another outlet for our creative energies, remains to be seen, but the trend is positive and encouraging: if *we* can do it, then others can as well, thus reducing the attraction of mass violence as an outlet for social energy.

In thinking about human violence, it is important to understand the difference between peace and stasis. Peace does not mean that we abandon the creative drives that led to stunning advances in medicine, social justice, and the arts. Even if we wanted to, this would be an unrealistic goal since human beings are naturally restless creatures who will always seek new frontiers. However, those frontiers need not be violent ones. Our task is to craft a social system that allows our energies to be used for creative purposes rather than destructive ones. Peace, like humanity, is dynamic.

Combining the themes of this chapter with our previous observations on human nature suggests that we really *can* reduce the probability of future mass violence. The relatively low rate of murder in most developed countries suggests that we are not intrinsically violent, but the alarming rate of violence in wars and in genocide suggests that we have the *potential* to kill when we associate in large groups. Our human nature is less at fault in causing mass violence than the social systems that we have devised to help us live together.

The encouraging news is that strong democratic governments have reduced *both* individual homicides and state-sponsored violence. Experience shows that the domestic murder rate is lower in societies with strong central governments, especially those with a workable judiciary that can resolve disagreements short of violence. And so far, no two democracies have gone to war with one another. While we have only a few centuries of experience with functioning democracies, the trend is positive and suggests that if more countries had this type of government, then the world would be a safer place. The problem is that not every country is ready for the introduction of a liberal democracy. It took time for the details of representative government to be worked out in England, France, and even in the United States, so it would be naïve to expect that we could transplant this experience lock, stock, and barrel into countries with no history of responsible government, ones where the educational level is too low to permit the engagement of the population on the issues. Our challenge is to design a process where the benefits of representative government can be made available to more people in a systematic way, to create peaceful outlets for our natural restlessness, and in so doing to *consciously design ways to reduce the probability of future mass violence.*

As obvious as this might sound, it is remarkable that so little attention has been given to the problem of reducing large-scale violence. We have programs to end poverty, reduce illiteracy, and eliminate preventable diseases, yet we spend almost nothing on planning ways to prevent large wars. Glenn Paige, a retired professor of political science, makes this point in his book *Nonkilling Global Political Science*, the publication of which is a story in itself.

Paige is an intense man with a passion for nonviolence. With the slightly rumpled look of a scholar, he is a veteran of the Korean War and has seen the ugliness of large-scale violence first hand. Ever since he returned from Korea, he has wondered why it is that we, as intelligent beings, seem not only to tolerate war but to glorify it. With leanings on the scientific side of political science, he deviated from the well-trodden field of the causes of war to study what makes for *peace*. He was surprised, after the carnage of the twentieth century, that his preliminary investigations were met with little enthusiasm from his professional peers. So far did he venture outside the mainstream of academic political science that he had to publish his most recent book using his own funds.

Paige is an idealist to be sure, but he is one who understands that violence has a strong grip on our society. His first goal was to simply understand why war was such an accepted social institution in the civilized world. Why is it, he asks, that almost all papers, books, and university dissertations on war and peace seem to focus on the causes of war, the conduct of war, and the results of war? Why is it that so few give that same degree of attention to the causes of peace, the conduct of peace, and the results of peace? It really is curious that we spend so much time wringing our hands over violence in the world and so little time thinking of ways to prevent it. Why doesn't the eradication of mass violence have the same priority as the eradication of mass poverty? Contrary to expectation, Paige's book has gained a wide international following. It has already been translated into twenty-two languages and he is constantly on the road to promote its message. Many of his trips are to the world's trouble spots, places where mass violence is a reality that people have to deal with every day. They are tired of the killing and are looking for a way out.

Over the past century we have learned more about ourselves and the social institutions in which we live than we did during the fifty centuries that separate us from the Sumerian king list. We have tried a wide range of social systems, from the divine right of kings to communism, and have found that democracy seems to work best at reducing both large- and small-scale violence. And we have come to realize that we are a restless species, one with a strong internal drive to expand and explore new frontiers. Now is the time to put that knowledge and experience to work so that we do not repeat the mistakes of our past, mistakes that will be ever more deadly as the ability to destroy leaves the domain of the major nation-states and proliferates across the globe. However, wherever we choose to go, we start from where we are today, which is our next topic to consider.

THREE | a realistic assessment of the world we live in

It was the best of times, it was the worst of times. —CHARLES DICKENS

The cold war had been over just long enough for the euphoria to wear off and for worry to set in. What were the Russians up to in their secret nuclear cities that appeared on no maps yet housed hundreds of thousands of people? Where were those cryptic mailing addresses that received trainloads of scientific equipment and had "red border" priority on every requisition, the laboratories that had created the immense and powerful Soviet nuclear arsenal? Were they developing a new generation of weapons for the defense of their motherland or were they negotiating with Iran, China, or North Korea for the sale of their special skills? Times were tough and fences built to keep out spies now kept out the wave of reform that was sweeping across Russia; scientists who were once privileged members of Soviet society were now planting potatoes to keep food on their tables.

Early in 1992, Sig Hecker, the director of Los Alamos, proposed a simple but effective solution to the mystery: "Why don't we just go ask them?" Los Alamos had designed most of the U.S. nuclear arsenal and there was a chance that the Russians might talk to a delegation of technical experts. The Department of Energy approved Hecker's suggestion and two high-level exchange visits, one in each country, were quickly arranged for the spring of that year. During the Russian visit to Los Alamos, I was impressed by the talk of a short bald man from the secret city of Arzamas-16 (the Russian Los Alamos), a man who described in one hour a lifetime of research covering just about every branch of physics. I was intrigued by his unique combination of creativity and practicality; not only did he speculate on many fascinating ideas—such as how one might create a magnetic field millions of times more powerful than that of Earth—he showed slide after slide of photographs and results. I decided then and there that I had to work with him, and a few months later I accompanied a team of scientists to Moscow to hammer out a list of potential topics for cooperation, a list that each side could then present to its government for approval. As it happened, Alexander Pavlovsky, the man who had given the impressive talk at Los Alamos, was to be the principal on the Russian side and I was nominated for the American side. In December 1992, when we were near to an agreement on the first phase of the work, the news came that the man whom I had come to know as Sasha had suffered a heart attack and died.

So there I stood in a cold Russian cemetery, holding a wreath inscribed with "From your American colleagues." My Russian hosts helped me to add it to the already huge mound of flowers on the grave and then, quite on impulse, I knelt down in the snow, removed my hat, and bowed my head. I did it to pay tribute to a brave man whom I also respected as a great scientist. What I didn't know was that the local television station was filming the event and that tens of thousands of Russians would see it on the evening news. Pavlovsky was a member of the Russian Academy of Sciences, a giant in Russian physics who could stare down a KGB officer and call the president if he didn't like the way things were going in the country. But he knew that he was risking his life to push for interactions with the Americans. Should a conservative regime replace the liberal one currently in power, he could expect to be dragged from his house in the middle of the night, never to be seen or heard from again. He also knew that Russia had to change: to remain a closed society was to risk being left behind. More than respected, Pavlovsky was truly loved as someone who took care of his people, a scientist of exceptional vision and talent, one who could compete with the Americans and come out on top over and over again. To see a senior American nuclear weapons scientist kneeling at his grave made a strong impression on the Russians.

But not everyone was favorably impressed. That evening, a formal dinner was held in the House of Scientists at Arzamas-16, a sort of clubhouse for senior staff at the laboratory. My new counterpart was introduced to me as Yuri Trutnev, a dynamic bear of a man whose seventy years had produced not a single gray hair, a tough guy of the old school. Though virtually unknown in the West, he had worked closely with Andrei Sakarov and invented many key concepts in Soviet nuclear weapons. The dinner began badly. The initial toasts were cold and formal, with little of the warmth that characterized a typical Russian meal. While I was giving the first American toast, full of good wishes and hopes that someday we might work together for the good of all humankind, Trutnev sat slouched beside me loudly humming the American national anthem. "You don't belong here. There is no reason for you to be here other than to steal Russian know-how," he told me after I sat down. Realizing that it was now or never, I began to lay out my argument for why Russian and American nuclear weapons specialists should at least begin a dialogue. We who had invented the most destructive objects ever created now had the responsibility to work together for a new future. I wasn't interested in a one-off visit or in buying Russian technology at fire-sale prices. I was proposing that we work together side by side, as equals. More than that, I understood the dangers of working in areas that brushed up against state secrets and proposed that we adopt a step-by-step policy wherein we would start with very simple things like exchanging published papers and gradually build confidence toward doing significant (unclassified, non-weapons-related) work together. Perhaps one day we would be doing collaborative experiments, each side contributing what it was best at to solve some particularly difficult problem in pure science. I could tell that Trutnev was interested because every time I tried to raise a forkful of food to my mouth he would grab my arm to emphasize a point. (Yuri is nothing if not enthusiastic.) Over the course of a couple of hours, he went from cynic to supporter, and the lab-to-lab program of collaboration was established. Every time I met Yuri afterward I received a crushing Russian hug.

In the ensuing years, scores of joint experiments were conducted. Russian claims of technical capability, once discounted as incredible propaganda, were verified by American instruments. By combining our skills, we accomplished feats that neither side could have done by itself. We produced some of the highest magnetic fields ever recorded and used them to do precise measurements of the properties of materials. We wrote computer codes to analyze the structure of proteins. Novel tests of the theory of superconductors were conducted by an international consortium of five countries, with the United States and Russia in the lead. We started a program to help Russia protect its nuclear material, an effort that has grown tremendously and that now stretches across Russia, keeping dangerous materials out of the hands of terrorists. All of this work was unclassified and all of it was published to show the world that former adversaries were now working together. It was our way of showing that the cold war really was over, that the very people who had constructed the massive arsenals that threatened global destruction were turning their talents to peaceful pursuits, and that they were doing it together in an open and verifiable way.

Perhaps most important, scientists on both sides got to know and trust one another. They told us about their suffering and sacrifices during World War II and their fear of the United States, a country that they saw as an avowed enemy of communism and one that had demonstrated a frightening new superweapon. We told them of our worries about the future of Russia, pressing them to be careful about who they talked to, since the United States was concerned that vital Russian secrets could fall into the wrong hands. Sometimes our advice had an effect. On the last morning of a trip to Arzamas-16, I was summoned to the director's office. Smiling while he opened a bottle of cognac, he said that he wanted to thank me. "For what?" I asked. "You kept us out of the hands of the Chinese," he replied. It seemed that other Russian institutes had accepted offers of help from the East and were rewarded with large-scale espionage. Arzamas-16 chose wisely.

At the end of the cold war, policy experts spoke of a "strategic pause," a period in which the international order was being reshuffled as a consequence of the breakup of the Soviet Union. There was an almost audible global sigh of relief as the threat of a massive nuclear exchange between the United States and the Soviet Union receded into history. People in Eastern Europe were giddy with a freedom untasted in generations. The reunification of Germany went from a dream to a reality. But the fizz was not out of the celebratory champagne before the effects of long-suppressed hatred began to emerge. Yugoslavia split into pieces with a brutality that shocked the world. Smoldering African civil wars flared up with the introduction of cheap weapons smuggled or bought openly from the former Soviet Union. North Korea flouted the international community by testing new long-range missiles. Terrorism moved from a few extremists hiding from the police to thousands of zealots training in Afghanistan. *What happened?* How did that good will, that enthusiasm for a new beginning, that optimism for the future, evaporate so quickly? The terrorist attacks of September 11, 2001, were certainly a proximate cause of later trouble, but perhaps there was something deeper, something more fundamental that caused the promise of long-term peace to evaporate before our eyes.

Few international arrangements are without any merit and that includes the superpower confrontation that dominated the second half of the twentieth century. Not discounting the frightening possibility that the cold war could have turned hot, with the loss of hundreds of millions of people, the standoff between East and West had the positive effect of restraining some countries from doing bad things. The threat of economic sanctions from Washington or the appearance of a column of Russian tanks in an East European capital put many a potential miscreant back in his box, nipping tensions in the bud. True, the Soviets and the Chinese supported North Korea and North Vietnam in bloody regional wars, just as we supported South Korea and South Vietnam, but neither side seriously thought of introducing nuclear weapons and both sides understood that there were limits beyond which they had best not trespass.

With the end of the cold war, some of those restraints were suddenly removed, and governments that had previously been in the orbits of Washington and Moscow felt free to do whatever they pleased, no matter how destructive to themselves or their neighbors. It seems unlikely that the ethnic violence that erupted in Yugoslavia would have been tolerated during Soviet times; it remains to be seen whether the breakup of that country into tiny independent states will be a net benefit to their populations. But lest one wax nostalgic for the comfortable bilateral stability of the cold war, remember that the superpower confrontation didn't prevent genocide in Cambodia, civil war in Angola, or the bloody Iran-Iraq War, all cases where the local governments correctly calculated that neither superpower would intervene. It is also unclear whether either superpower would have interfered in the civil war and foreign incursions that later claimed *4 million lives* in the Congo. We worried about terrorism less during the cold war, but perhaps that was only because it lacked a leader or a cause. Finally, remember that during the Cuban missile crisis the Soviet Union and United States very nearly came to thermonuclear blows.

Vic Reis likes to show a chart of the number of people killed in wars over the past two hundred years, a curve that rises almost exponentially until 1945 and the invention of the atomic bomb. After that, there were a series of "local wars" but no devastating world war that resulted in tens of millions of deaths. He does this to demonstrate that, for all their destructive potential, nuclear weapons really did create a pause in, or even put a stop to, the seeming inexorable rise in deaths due to warfare. A strategic planner by nature, Vic can focus on an idea like a laser beam, repeating a message over and over until it becomes the commonly accepted view, using his quick wit to disarm critics and to charm allies. In 1993, he took over as assistant secretary of energy for Defense Programs, the head of all nuclear weapons activities in the country, and immediately set to work reforming a bu-reaucracy struggling to adapt to a changing world. Never one for big meetings or the protracted debate typical of government, he pur-posefully chose conference rooms that held only four or five people, inviting only those who had the authority and ability to make things happen. As head of the weapons program at Los Alamos during the mid-1990s, I spent endless hours working with Vic to lay out a new strategy for nuclear weapons, one that did not rely on explosive test-ing, but one that would assure the safety and reliability of our arsenal for as long as we needed it. It was a bold plan for its time, and Vic can take credit for reversing a crash-dive in the budget of the American nuclear weapons program that threatened to effectively disarm us by the end of the decade. But we now know that the changes in the world were so great that even the creative ideas developed in those little conference rooms missed the mark by a mile. The world was changing in very fundamental ways and the old toolsets that we re-lied on—powerful weapons and their ability to deter or to win major wars—were becoming historical anachronisms as curious as moats around stone castles. The wars of the future were going to be differ-ent, so different that the very word "war" would hardly describe their complexity.

Human beings derive part of their self-image from the groups that they belong to and part from those that they *oppose.* Upon losing the superpower standoff as the focus of their opposition, governments found something else to take its place, sometimes, as in the case of Yugoslavia, resurrecting centuries-old grudges, and sometimes, as in the case of organized global terrorism, inventing brand-new causes. This doesn't mean that any single individual or group woke up one morning and decided that there were too few villains in the world and that they would have to step up to the role. Nor does it imply that simmering tensions boiled over when the restraining lid of superpower domination was removed, that people were just biding their time before acting up. But it does appear from history that long periods of tension-free international peace are exceeding rare. Whether consciously or unconsciously, human beings act so as to ensure that an adversarial relationship is maintained, and if that relationship goes away, another is quickly invented to take its place. If we don't *consciously* decide to set up an adversary then we seem to unconsciously act toward the same end.

Not everything in the world happens as a result of clear rational thinking, an optimization of benefits and a minimization of costs. Do you wake up in the morning and do a nutritional analysis of what you would like to have for breakfast, calculate whether it is more efficient to put gas in the car on the way to work or on the way home, or decide the optimum flow of work on your desk? Most people don't, instead relying on snap decisions, intuition, or just plain habit to guide them through the routine tasks of the day. An analogous thing happens in society when a large number of people seem to spontaneously decide something, be it around fashion or a political cause. Sociologists call this phenomenon "emergent behavior," a distinct action of a group resulting from seemingly uncorrelated individual decisions. Have you ever been in a meeting when, after a long and complex discussion, it suddenly dawns on everyone that the solution is right in front of them? Or, have you ever clung to an outdated idea because everyone else did? Even the most dispassionate scientists get caught up in defending theories that are past their prime, as Einstein did when he resisted quantum mechanics because it seemed too messy compared to the elegance of classical physics. In its violent form, emergent behavior is mob behavior, a type of mass hysteria in which otherwise reasonable and good people commit acts of violence that they would never contemplate on their own. Emergent behaviors also happen at the international level and sometimes get out of control, one thing building on another until something occurs that nobody wanted. Wars have started this way.

Two things suggest that the future international order could be much more complex than anything we have seen in the recent past. First, the disappearance of the spheres of influence of the superpowers has taken a discipline out of the international arena, a discipline that suppressed many smaller conflicts before they got started. Second, the proliferation of weapons of mass destruction has the potential to make future conflicts far more dangerous than previous ones. Whereas in the past a relatively small set of major powers, those with large standing armies, nuclear weapons, and economic might, occupied most of our attention, in the future we will have to give almost the same level of consideration to many more countries, especially those that possess or threaten to develop weapons of mass destruction. And it's more than a worry for the distant future—the border dispute in Kashmir assumed a whole new dimension when India and Pakistan each demonstrated a nuclear capability. No longer was this just a local matter, an annual exchange of artillery shells and raiding parties. Should one side achieve unexpected success on the ground, it is possible that the other side might panic and respond with nuclear weapons. Millions would die. (Fortunately, after crossing the nuclear threshold, the leaders of both of these countries seemed to recognize that they were playing with nuclear fire and began to explore measures that would lessen tensions.)

Something equally frightening could happen in one of the frequent disputes between African countries. While regional wars in Africa receive little press in the developed world, that would quickly change the first time one of those conflicts involved a virulent and contagious biological weapon. It is highly likely that the pathogen would spread out of its initial area of application, turning a regional problem into a global one.

While they should be a principal focus of concern, weapons of mass destruction are not the only worry. Four million people died in the Congo's civil war, which was fought with secondhand guns and knives. This is twice as many deaths as would result from a nuclear exchange between India and Pakistan. Just think about the determination required to kill so many using only light weapons—and what that same determination would do with far more capable weapons of mass destruction. Would the governments of those countries suddenly become more responsible once they acquired such weapons, less willing to commit violence? I doubt it.

Since the end of the cold war, we have moved from bipolar stability to multipolar complexity. Let's look at some specific countries and try to project where they might go in the next decade or two. I'll start with some of the most powerful countries to explain why I think that their attentions will be mainly directed toward domestic issues and will then turn to some of the more problematic developing countries.

Let us look first at Russia, which is one of the two countries in the world (the United States is the other) with enough nuclear weapons to end civilization as we know it. Like most complex countries, just about everything that you can say about Russia is true, along with its converse. Russia is huge—stretching over eleven time zones—but it has a population only half that of the United States. Russia maintains an enormous nuclear arsenal but is barely able to keep its army fed and clothed. It is arrogant in promoting its own high culture but xenophobic about foreigners coming in to steal its best and brightest. When the cold war ended, many people said that Russia would take a generation or more to recover, if it could recover at all. But less than two decades later Russia appears to be making a rapid comeback, as it has so many times in the past. For example, at the turn of the twentieth century, Russia was forging ahead in converting a feudal economy into a modern nation—it had some of the most extensive telephone and railway networks in Europe and was a rising manufacturing power. After suffering huge losses in World War I and greater losses in the revolution, Russia rebuilt its armed forces so that by the late 1930s—half a generation later—it had the largest (though not the best in quality) air force in the world. After suffering 20 million dead in World War II and the destruction of many of its largest cities, the Soviet Union rebuilt its technical base and, in 1949, detonated its own atomic bomb, years ahead of Western intelligence estimates. Even more impressive, in 1957—half a generation after the end of the war—it was able to launch Sputnik, the world's first artificial satellite. Russia has the quality of a boxer who, after being relentlessly pummeled by his opponent, continues to stand and hold his ground. And it's more than spirit: Russia is blessed with enormous reserves of natural resources and has a well-educated and relatively disciplined population; there is great opportunity, if only that opportunity can be harnessed.

When President Vladimir Putin came to power he inherited a crumbling state rife with corruption, a country bleeding to death as people and treasure fled to safe havens abroad. Tough, skillful, and determined, he has systematically taken hold of the reins of power to bring the country back to the right, hardly a surprising course, since Russia has, for a thousand years, always gone back to strong central leadership after a period of change and liberalization. Putin's steps were quite predictable: First, ensure the structural integrity of the country by getting control of the *oblasts*, the regions that, under Boris Yeltsin, had threatened to declare their autonomy, or even their outright independence, from Moscow. Second, get control of the media so that the people will hear only one set of messages, freeing the government from the need to debate complex and necessary policies. Third, gain control of the money that was converting the natural wealth of the country into foreign bank accounts for a few oligarchs. Fourth, get control of the military and reshape it to serve the needs of a new Russia in a new world, an instrument of influence as well as defense. Even the most ardent supporters of democracy in Russia will see analogies between Putin and Lenin, even Putin and the tsars. What's the next step? How about a dose of xenophobia, blaming the West for engineering the collapse of the Soviet Union and announcing the need for sacrifices to help rebuild Mother Russia? This would be an easy sell, since two-thirds of Russians already believe that the Western nations undermined the Soviet Union.

Whatever he does, President Putin faces daunting problems. Russia's population is in steady decline, and is expected to drop from its current value of just below 150 million to only 80 to 100 million by 2020. This is due to a low birthrate, poor health care, and high levels of alcoholism, smoking, bad diet, and stress. A smaller population implies a smaller internal market for goods and services and a reduced ability to produce goods for export. Another problem is that, for the first time, the Russians have a pretty good idea of what the rest of the world is like. Under the tsars and under communism, most Russians believed that they lived at least as well as people in other countries. Now they watch Western TV shows and are avid surfers of the Internet. They know how other people live and have no desire to return to a time of long lines and poor quality. On the international front, Russia is wary of neighboring Central Asian countries ruled by petty dictators, some of whom sit on massive reserves of oil and other natural resources. It has been fighting an internal war with Chechnya since 1994, and there is potential trouble with other regions and groups as well. Despite these daunting problems, Russia's history of recovering from the most devastating events makes it unwise to count it out. Barring catastrophe, always a core competence of Russian governments, I think that Russia will reemerge on the international stage, demanding respect and flexing its muscle. However, its problems are sufficient to suggest that most of the country's energies will be focused internally rather than directed to a course of empire building or power projection. For one thing, it will take time to rebuild the Russian army and navy to competitive standards. And the Russian people, while heroically patient, will not wait forever for improvements in their living conditions.

No discussion of world affairs could long delay a look at China. Everything about this country is fantastic. It is the world's most populous state, with more than 1.2 billion people. It has enjoyed near double digit economic growth for over a decade. Its breakneck construction program consumes over one-third of all the concrete produced in the world. The list could go on for pages. One is hard-pressed to buy anything not manufactured or assembled in China, from coffee mugs (the CIA's mugs are made there) to computer security cards (the password cards used to gain access to Los Alamos computers were made there too).

Unlike Russia, China seems to be managing the transition to a market economy without the Communist central government losing its strong grip on society. Economic reform in China has encouraged foreign investment, and this, combined with vast natural resources and a huge internal market for local production, suggests to some analysts that China's economy could exceed that of the United States within two or three decades. However, there are several reasons why such projections of China's potential might be a bit too rosy.

First, China faces a massive demographic problem that could seriously impede its ability to sustain rapid growth. Fearing a population explosion that might have led to widespread famine and hardship, the Chinese government implemented a strict one-child policy for couples, the penalties for violation being quite severe. The population did stabilize and has remained within the country's ability to feed and house, but the result is a large and growing number of older citizens who expect to live many years into retirement. Lacking a social security system, the cost of supporting this aging population falls to the limited number of sons (daughters are not required to support their parents) who are called on to support their own immediate families, two sets of parents, and any other close relatives. It is hard to save money, become a conspicuous consumer, or buy a house under such a crushing burden.

A second challenge to China lies in its huge agrarian population. Most Chinese people live in the countryside where jobs and social services are scarce to nonexistent. They are beginning to ask why workers in Beijing and Shanghai have good schools and modern hospitals while peasants in the countryside struggle with poorly trained teachers and long waits at second-rate clinics. Integrating hundreds of millions of rural people into an increasingly urban and technological culture will be a challenge to even the most creative policy makers.

Finally, one of the more tricky problems that China will have to face is how to effect a transition from rapid development to the sustainable growth of an established economic power. It is one thing to use low-priced labor to manufacture goods for export; it is quite another to adjust to saturating markets, lower-priced competitors, and global economic downturns. Japan, for all its economic savvy, was

unable to prevent a near meltdown in its economy as it lost manufacturing jobs while artificially inflated Tokyo real estate values shot
through the roof. How China deals with its own version of this challenge remains to be seen.

I believe that China will most likely remain focused on internal
matters for some years to come. While a future Chinese government
certainly might use the return of Taiwan to mainland control as an
excuse to divert attention from domestic issues, that would be done
in the context of an uncertain U.S. response and the possibility that
Taiwan could, at some future date, develop its own nuclear weapons
to balance the mainland's advantage in troops and aircraft. China
wants and deserves respect on the international stage and correctly
calculates that it can more easily gain that respect through peaceful
means than by threats of aggression.

What about Europe? A century ago Europe would have dominated
any discussion of international relations—it claimed ownership of
most of the world and it had powerful armies and navies to back up
that claim. However, after two devastating world wars, Europe is
wary of any tension that could lead to renewed continental conflict.
Indeed, the direction of European politics is strongly focused on the
type of economic integration and common policy that would make
warfare between member states almost unthinkable. Demographic
problems related to aging populations, falling birthrates, and rising
immigration are also causing Europe to concentrate more on internal issues than on external ones. Italy has a zero or slightly negative
birthrate, implying that its population will decrease over the coming
years, reducing the internal market for everything from food to films.
Germany is facing wrenching decisions on the reduction of gener-
ous social programs as the number of retired people exceeds the car-

rying capacity of the working population. France is in the throes of rising social tension as increasing numbers of immigrants openly flout local customs, making some French feel like a minority in their own country. Europe will continue to take a responsible role in international affairs, but because of the many internal challenges, the major European nations will likely stay focused on domestic issues for some time.

I have left the United States for last in our discussion of major nations because we are, quite simply, in an incredibly strong position militarily, economically, and culturally. The United States currently has overwhelming military superiority—we can win any conventional battle, anywhere, anytime. We have the largest economy on Earth and the dollar remains the standard by which all other currencies are judged. American culture, much to the chagrin of foreign elites, dominates the world.

Perhaps the most fundamental reason for optimism about the future of the United States is that, in contrast to Russia and Europe, the population of the United States continues to increase by births and by immigration. We have both the people to invent the goods of the future and the internal market to consume them. While it's true that manufacturing jobs have been migrating from country to country as companies seek lower costs, the intellectual power that creates those industries often resides in the United States. Our agricultural productivity means that we can easily feed more people and, despite having our own problems with the assimilation of immigrants and minorities, we are still proud of being a melting pot of cultures, religions, and ethnicities.

We certainly have our problems—one need only think of the rising gap between rich and poor, the drug problem, rising health care costs, continued worries over the quality of our schools. But compared to other countries, we are in astonishingly good shape. And it is more than just national pride that makes me say this. Think about how many people struggle to get to the United States and acquire legal immigrant status, scrimping and saving to bring their families here. How many people are as anxious to get to China, Russia, Germany, or Japan? We have a reputation as a place where anyone can succeed, where a poor child can grow up to be president, where ability rather than family history is still the dominant factor in individual success, and where people are generally left in peace to live their lives.

The biggest challenge faced by the United States is how to deal with our position as the sole remaining superpower—what French observers call the "hyperpower." The events of the twentieth century thrust us into a prominence that we were neither seeking nor well prepared to accept. Through the misty lens of history, it seems obvious that we would ride to the rescue of Europe in the two World Wars, but at the time there were strong contingents that saw those conflicts as none of our business and certainly not worth the lives of our sons and daughters. Even today we debate our failure to act more promptly in Rwanda, Kosovo, and the Sudan. We do care about people in far-off places, but we think that they should be able to solve their own problems without our interference. The fundamental error that Osama bin Laden made in attacking the United States was that he took this as an indication that we lacked the backbone for a fight; he failed to understand that prescient comment of Admiral Yamamoto of Japan, who, after the attack on Pearl Harbor, said that Japan had "awakened a sleeping giant."

As the most powerful country on Earth, what can the United States do to reduce the probability of mass violence in the future? What should we avoid doing? No other country enjoys the freedom of action that we enjoy, and no other country will have such a profound effect on the future as the United States. How we use this power is the issue at hand, and the topic of the last third of this book.

Now let's look at the rest of the world, the part that has the majority of the people, the highest birthrate, the worst poverty, and the most dangerous combination of old ethnic hatreds and new unproven governments.

With over 1 billion people, India is the second most populous country in the world and the world's largest democracy. Pakistan, formed as a Muslim partition out of mainly Hindu India, is smaller and has oscillated between democracy and military dictatorship. In 1998, India and Pakistan each tested nuclear weapons, claiming they were essential to their national security. India has fought border wars with China, which has nuclear weapons. And Pakistan worries that if it doesn't have nuclear capability, India will use nuclear blackmail to force an unfavorable settlement in Kashmir. Despite a recent and welcome relaxation of tensions, many international observers think that conflict over Kashmir is the most likely spark for a nuclear war in the coming years. India and Pakistan understand the damage that would be inflicted by nuclear weapons, but neither has crafted a responsible policy to control them. Pakistan is in an especially difficult position: in the event of an invasion, it would have to use its nuclear arsenal at once because its cities are so close to the border. There would be no time for negotiations if the military situation turned against them.

Like China, India and Pakistan face daunting internal problems in bringing their rural poor—the majority of their populations—into line with the high-tech world. This goal is more than pure altruism on the part of the governments. India's ruling party, the BJP, was trounced in the 2004 elections when the rural vote sent the message that they were tired of waiting for better health care, higher-paying jobs, and quality education. Pakistan has its own problems dealing with radical Islamic fundamentalism, a movement which discourages education beyond the teaching of the Koran and this only to boys. (The principal of a religious school in Pakistan recently asked a visiting American official why the United States was persecuting Islam, adding that there was no evidence that Muslims were involved in any terrorist attacks. You can guess for yourself what the students are taught.) The very prospect of a fundamentalist Islamic government gaining possession of Pakistan's capable nuclear arsenal should send shivers down the spine of the most ardent optimist.

Many countries around the world are still struggling to rationalize borders that were arbitrarily laid down by former colonial powers. We are living with this problem today as we deal with ethnic divisions in Iraq, a former colony whose borders were hurriedly drawn in 1926 by an Anglo-French commission anxious to complete its task before the onset of brutal summer weather. Little consideration was given to ancient tribal, ethnic, and religious differences, between the Kurds in the north, the Arabs of central Iraq, and the southern Marsh Arabs.

Border disputes have always been a danger to peace, and even a quick look at a demographic map will reveal problems waiting to happen, situations where age-old adversaries mix within one country only to be split across international boundaries. The best example of the former is the dilemma faced by Israel and Palestine, both peoples claiming the same land as their ancestral right. Even a partition of territory, as was accomplished by splitting Pakistan from India, seems beyond agreement as Israelis continue to build settlements on land claimed by the Palestinians while Palestinians continue to conduct terrorist attacks within Israel. One is ever hopeful when a breath of moderation appears, only to have that hope swept away by the next provocation on one side or the other. An example of an ethnic split across international boundaries is the Kurdish population, divided between Turkey, Iran, and Iraq. None of these countries wants an independent Kurdistan (partly due to the loss of oil revenue) and all of them are worried about a violent insurgency within their borders.

Migration and religious conflicts are particularly vexing problems. Malaysia is only just managing to keep the lid on tensions resulting from the ethnic Chinese minority's economic dominance of the country, an affront to indigenous Malays who wonder why another ethnic group controls their ancestral homeland. Thailand is struggling to contain violence in the south as the local Muslim population chafes under regulations designed for the national Buddhist majority. Ethnic animosity simmers in the Balkans, and Central Asian nations are still coming to grips with how to handle the large ethnic Russian population descended from people forcibly relocated during Stalin's repopulation programs. Clearly the Malay government is not going to eject the Chinese minority, Thailand is not going to grant autonomy to its southern provinces, and millions of people are probably not going to be relocated to accomplish ethnic homogeneity in the Balkans and Central Asia. A peaceful resolution to any of these issues is possible, but so too is protracted sectarian violence that hardens positions and builds resentment for generations to come. Finding an equitable solution is exacerbated by the fact that many of the central governments are relatively new, the countries being just a few decades away from colonial rule or only just out of the oppressive grip of communism. They are still learning how to govern and the people are still learning what it means to be governed by responsible and representative governments.

What these governments need most is time—time to solve some of their most pressing problems, time to reach workable accommodations on those problems that they can't solve, and time to build a reputation for reliability with their own people and with other nations. Unfortunately, time is precisely what they don't have as events rush forward with a velocity that exceeds rational response. Not only must a government deal with its own people, who are now much better informed than ever before. It must also deal with external agitators who can reach its citizens via the Internet and satellite television and who can sir up discontent without ever setting foot in the country.

Added to the urgency of coming to grips with regional problems is the danger that one or more conflicts could cross the threshold from conventional warfare or terrorism to the use of weapons of mass destruction. As technology spreads around the world, bringing greater destructive power within range of nations and even small groups, there is a real possibility that one or both sides may resort to chemical, biological, or even nuclear weapons. And it is not only attacks from other countries that are of concern. The ease with which a domestic terrorist group might gain access to biological agents or industrial chemicals means that a small number of people could wreak havoc within their own country. This is a new thing—something that would have been impossible twenty years ago but which is frighteningly real today. The anthrax attack on the U.S. Senate and the nuclear weapons programs of Iran and Libya are clear indicators that these technologies are within the reach of those who would have and use them. Iraq used chemical weapons in the war it fought against Iran. Suppose that in a future war the Iranians succeeded in their drive to create even a primitive nuclear weapon? Maybe possession of such powerful weapons would cause governments to moderate their behavior, but history is certainly not encouraging on this point.

The international order is crossing a fundamental threshold, comparable to the one crossed by individual human beings when a sling, spear, or bow allowed a small person to kill a much larger, much stronger person. Just as physical strength was no longer the sole determinant of success in individual combat, conventional military or economic might will no longer be the sole determinants of influence in international affairs. A carrier battle group is no match for even a primitive nuclear weapon, and the threat of economic sanctions may ring hollow if a vial of lethal biological pathogens is slipped into the presidential soup. Just as civil society developed ways to deal with an individual's potential to kill, so too will international society have to learn how to control the increased destructive capability that will soon be available to almost anyone who wants it. In the case of the individual, it took millennia of experimentation to arrive at a social system that effectively suppressed homicide. Now we are faced with the same challenge in the society of nations—but we do not have millennia to find a solution.

Given the complexity of group behavior, is there any hope of moderating future mass violence, especially when weapons of mass destruction are spreading beyond the major powers? Is human society so complex as to defy control, a lethal combination of the quixotic nature of individual human beings and the complex systems that we use to organize ourselves? There is no magic solution to managing world affairs, some perfect system that, once implemented, would allow all humanity to live in peace and freedom, a metaphorical riding off into the sunset. Because after the sun sets, it rises again on new people with new needs and aspirations. Humanity is constantly changing, and with it the emergent behavior that it produces. Our task is not to pine for some halcyon past or to resist change but to look at the changes that will inevitably occur, seize opportunities as they arise, and avoid those things that our experience tells us could lead to mass violence.

Referring to her hometown, Oakland, Gertrude Stein once re-marked, "There is no there there." There is no end to history or to our struggle to live in peace. The future is a journey, not a destina-tion, and it is likely that we will be as worried about the potential for mass violence a century from now as we are today. Our goal is to identify practical policies that will reduce the rate of large-scale vio-lence in a manner analogous to the way that laws and police forces reduced the number of domestic homicides. A discussion of some of these practical ideas will occupy the last part of this book, but to allay suspicions of proposals for a new world government or the enlightenment of humanity, let me say that both of these things have been tried and neither worked very well. What we will do is take a hard look at what *has* and *has not* worked in the spheres of diplomacy, economics, and military affairs—all in the context of our imperfect and restless human nature—and try to learn from that experience to reduce the probability of making the same mistakes again. As always, we are moving into uncharted territory—the future—but we needn't be, and cannot allow ourselves to be, slaves to the basest elements of our nature. We can and we must do better.

PART II | the limits of choice:
how technology and culture
will affect our future

two technologies that will shape the world

The human mind is inspired enough when
it comes to inventing horrors; it is when it
tries to invent a Heaven that it shows itself
cloddish. —EVELYN WAUGH

I grew up in the 1950s, a time of implicit faith in the goodness of progress. It seemed that almost anything could be justified in terms of this guiding social principle, from bulldozing a pristine landscape to build a superhighway to using chemicals to boost farm productivity. The United States had won World War II with a combination of heroism, stunning scientific advances, and unparalleled industrial output. We had confidence that the future would be better than the past and that, by our labors, we would create that future. At trade shows and world's fairs, General Electric featured the all-electric House of the Future, complete with robot vacuum cleaners and an electric sidewalk de-icer. Such labor-saving devices would give us more time to spend with our families and enjoy life. General Motors thought that by now we would have room-sized automatic cars in which the driver would sit facing backwards in a comfortable living room setting, replete with paper and pipe and two happy children playing on the floor. Some of us would be colonizing the moon, or even Mars, and space travel would be as ho-hum as domestic flights.

Somewhere between the 1950s and today, the bloom seems to have come off the rose. Progress is now recognized as something that carries its own set of challenges and regrets and hardly something that is inexorable. Superhighways have lessened the time to get from place to place—unless you are trying to get there during rush hour. And it is a matter of opinion whether office automation and the revolution in telecommunications have made us more productive or just more frantic. Americans spend less time with their families today than they did twenty years ago and a recent study revealed that many workers feel guilty about taking even a week or two of vacation per year, believing that they are somehow letting their colleagues down—or, even worse, they fear that in their absence the company might realize that it could do just fine without them. Sometimes we wonder who is serving whom—whether technology is serving people or people are serving technology, captives to e-mail, cell phones, and pagers.

There is still a deeply held belief in the inevitability of progress, especially in Western society. My colleagues in the scientific community sometimes insist that all knowledge is inherently good and that every line of research *must* be followed to see where it leads. I have never agreed with that position. We might want to *know about* something, to understand what is possible and what is impossible, but to *do* something counter to our best interest is just plain stupid.

Deciding the issue of "best interest" can be tricky. During my career, I have terminated several projects that I believed crossed the gray line from ethical to questionable. One was the development of a laser blinder for use on the battlefield, a weapon that would blind opposing troops without killing them. On the one hand, it seemed more humane to blind someone with a laser than to kill him with a bullet; on the other hand there seemed to be a more manifest cruelty in maiming someone than shooting them. What would you do? Remember, doing nothing—neither shooting nor blinding—would simply allow the attacker to kill you, so it's very much a case of the lesser of two evils.

A second program that I terminated before it really got underway, was a plan to use special types of microwaves to scramble the thinking of an opponent. The advantage was that this nonlethal weapon would merely incapacitate an adversary, making it unnecessary to kill or even physically injure him. Unfortunately, the risk of permanent brain damage was real. Also, it wasn't clear whether scrambling an attacker's thoughts would lead to more peaceful or more violent behavior. In any event, I decided to devote my organization's limited resources to other things.

Perhaps the most dramatic example of deciding not to do something was the decision to halt the deployment of the Superbomb—an incredibly powerful variant of the hydrogen bomb whose explosive force was measured in tens to hundreds of millions of tons of TNT. Although there was a technical attraction to the project—it was a particularly elegant bit of applied physics—there was no real military application for a weapon of such power. It would be able to destroy large cities at a single blow, but it was less efficient than using several smaller weapons, since it would expend most of its energy in the immediate vicinity of the fireball rather than distributing it over a wide area. After careful consideration, the Department of Defense decided to cancel the program. Just because it was *possible* did not mean that it was *desirable*, or even useful. This was one of the very few times that we decided not to build a more powerful weapon, stopping a process that has gone on since the first time that our ancestors picked up a tool to use in violence.

We look at science and technology today with a more jaundiced eye than we did in the 1950s and 1960s, having realized that almost anything can be used for both good and evil. Medicine can cure diseases or create new ones that could be used as weapons. Nuclear energy can reduce greenhouse gases but it can also be used in a weapon that can kill hundreds of thousands of people in a single explosion. Sometimes even the most benign things can be used to do harm. Witness the capability of a kitchen knife to slice our daily bread or to kill. While some things are unquestionably more suited to doing harm than others, we increasingly find that, more than the technology itself, it is our decisions on how we apply that technology that determine its benefits or risks. While an assault rifle is designed expressly to kill, that function might be seen in a different light if the rifle were used to defend a civilian population against a brutal invasion. As much as we might like to see every issue as black or white, most of the world is painted in myriad shades of gray.

In the Introduction, I suggested that we are in the process of crossing two fundamental thresholds—one relating to the proliferation of weapons of mass destruction and the other to the acceleration of global communication and transportation. The first is clearly a bad thing: it hardly seems like a good idea for *more* countries to have nuclear, chemical, and biological weapons (although some people seem to think that *their* country has a special need for them). But the second is an instance where even a good thing can have unforeseen consequences. In this chapter, I will elaborate on each of these developments.

Fifty years ago the weapons available to individuals, groups, or even small nations were too small to kill large numbers of people at one time. There was a limit on how much destruction any one group could cause. For example, terrorists might have been able to acquire enough high explosive to make a single 2,000-pound bomb and set it off in a crowded train station, killing several hundred people. But they did not have access to weapons that were powerful enough to threaten the survival of a nation—until today.

Fifty years ago only a major nation could field a large army or mount a massive aerial bombardment that could kill hundreds of thousands of people. The horrific battles of World War I involved hundreds of thousands of men and lasted days, weeks, even months. The fire-bombing raids conducted against Germany and Japan at the end of World War II, attacks that actually killed more people than the atom bombs, involved hundreds of long-range bombers, aircraft that were expensive to make and complex to maintain. Very few countries had the ability or the money to manufacture such weapons delivery systems.

With the advent of the atom bomb, the club of military super-states grew even more exclusive: first, the United States alone, then the Soviet Union, soon followed by the United Kingdom, France, and China. For a long time membership in the nuclear club remained at five. Israel has steadfastly refused to confirm or deny ownership of nuclear weapons, but it is generally accepted that they have had a capable and extensive atomic arsenal since the early 1970s. India exploded a single "peaceful" device in 1974. (Exactly what India meant by "peaceful" was never made clear, but the implication was that they did not intend to field their primitive design as a weapon.) During the 1990s and early in the present century, a significant expansion of the nuclear club took place, with some members exhibiting extraordinary irresponsibility in dealing with their newfound power. A. Q.

Kahn, a Pakistani scientist, parlayed his involvement in that country's program to become a sort of international broker of nuclear technology, selling almost anything that a prospective nuclear nation might need, from centrifuge parts to a complete design for a nuclear weapon. And, if a country lacked the ability to deliver a weapon once it had one, North Korea was more than happy to sell long-range missiles to anyone with the ready cash. By the end of the 1990s, technologies that were once the exclusive preserve of advanced nations were within reach of countries like Iraq, Iran, Libya, and North Korea. And it wasn't just the "bad guy" states that had an interest in nuclear weapons; Switzerland and Sweden, among others, have acknowledged flirting with their own nuclear programs.

However, it would be wrong to assume that nuclear weapons are now easy to make, that once the secret was out anyone could read the instruction book and make one with materials found around the house. I am constantly amazed when self-declared "nuclear weapons experts," many of whom have never seen a real nuclear weapon, hold forth on how easy it is to make a functioning nuclear explosive. In fact, and thank goodness, there are some significant challenges.

All the nuclear nations had problems in constructing their first nuclear explosive. During the Manhattan Project, the World War II effort to develop the first atomic bomb, the United States assembled the finest collection of scientists and engineers in history and gave them nearly unlimited resources to achieve their goal. The Soviet Union had spies in the American program who conveyed almost every technical detail of the bomb's design, but it still took the Soviets four years to produce their own nuclear explosion. And France, a modern industrial nation, had numerous failures in its early weapons program despite knowing that an atomic bomb was possible and despite intense efforts to obtain information from existing nuclear states. Not only is the physics of nuclear explosives complex and not taught in universities; nuclear weapons require a significant national infrastructure, including a reliable supply of electricity, the ability to fabricate precision equipment, and a scientific cadre capable of managing the many aspects of nuclear weapons design and construction.

There are three steps to making a nuclear weapon: First, you need special nuclear material, particular forms of uranium or plutonium. Second, you have to assemble that nuclear material into a workable explosive device. Third, you need to make the weapon rugged enough to endure delivery by aircraft or missile. Each of these tasks carries its own challenges to the would-be nuclear state or group.

The first challenge is to get a sufficient quantity of plutonium or uranium to enable a chain reaction to take place in the weapon. How much you need depends on the design of the weapon: more sophisticated weapons require less, and less sophisticated weapons require more. Without revealing any classified information, I can say that you need more than you could carry in your pocket but less than you could carry in the trunk of your car.

Weapons-grade uranium has to be separated from naturally occurring ore, a process typically involving thousands of precision centrifuges. Plutonium is an artificial element made in a nuclear reactor and then chemically separated from the reactor fuel. These are sophisticated operations that require factory-sized buildings, and it is for this reason that would-be nuclear terrorists have focused on getting nuclear materials from the black market rather than trying to make their own. Fortunately, there have been few reported thefts of nuclear materials (most of them from within the former Soviet Union) and all of them have been of small quantities, far less than is required for a weapon. However, it is possible that a determined group might accumulate a sufficient quantity bit by bit. Because nuclear materials are the essential element in any nuclear weapons program and because their manufacture has fairly clear signatures, the International Atomic Energy Agency (IAEA) spends most of its monitoring effort on this phase of the weapons development process.

Many commentators equate having nuclear materials with having a nuclear weapon—even Kim Jong Il of North Korea referred to his separated plutonium as his "nuclear deterrent"—but it is in fact only the first, though admittedly crucial, step toward a weapon. Nuclear weapons designers refer to the second phase of weapons development as the construction of a "device," a complex assembly of uranium, plutonium, high explosives, and other materials that will, when activated, produce a nuclear detonation. Like most prototypes, the first weapon produced by a country is typically handmade and rather delicate in its construction, hardly a sure thing by any means. That is how the United States, Great Britain, France, and Russia did it and I would be surprised if a developing country could do otherwise.

While it is true that one can obtain the general idea behind a rudimentary nuclear explosive from articles on the Internet, none of these sources has enough detail to enable the confident assembly of a real nuclear explosive. Think of it this way: Most people are pretty familiar with automobiles and there are any number of books and magazines giving details of their design and manufacture. But if I were to deliver a ton of steel to your garage, along with some glass and plastic, could you make a car on your own using only hand tools? I doubt it. There are many tricks of the trade that even the most complete set of instructions won't contain, a fact apparent to anyone who has ever tried to follow the instructions for a complex do-it-yourself project. And you need more than machine tools to do it. You need a working knowledge of how the parts fit together, what tolerances are permitted or required, the compatibility of materials (for example, you can't weld some metals together), and many other details.

To be more specific, uranium is a material so hard that it is used in armor-piercing tank ammunition. It is exceptionally difficult to machine. Plutonium is one of the most complex metals ever discovered, a material whose basic properties are sensitive to exactly how it is processed. Both need special machining technology that has evolved though a process of trial and error. Another challenge to the would-be nuclear power is how to choose the right tolerances. "Just put a slug of uranium into a gun barrel and shoot it into another slug of uranium" is one description of how easy it is to make a nuclear explosive. However, if the gap between the barrel and the slug is too tight, then the slug may stick as it is accelerated down the barrel. If the gap is too big, then other, more complex, issues may arise. All of these problems can be solved by experimentation, but this experimentation requires a level of technical resources that, until recently, few countries had. How do you measure the progress of an explosive detonation without destroying the equipment doing the measurements? How do you perform precision measurements on something that only lasts a fraction of a millionth of a second?

Even advanced industrial nations had a remarkably difficult time solving problems that seem "obvious" to the experienced weapons designer. During a tour of a foreign nuclear weapons museum, I asked one of the designers why they took a particular design path, one that added a lot of extra weight to the weapon but nothing to its performance. "We didn't know any better," was the reply. Claims occasionally made in the newspaper that there is no need to classify nuclear weapons information because "everybody knows it already" are simply false.

As an example of the challenges faced by recent nuclear proliferants, consider the weapons programs of India and Pakistan. India tested a nuclear device in 1974; photographs show a large device typical of first-time nuclear designs. Over the years, Indian scientists worked hard to understand how nuclear weapons work, using scientific data in the open literature to refine their computer codes and improve their predictions. They felt confident enough to make the jump from an atomic bomb—one that utilizes the principle of nuclear fission—to a hydrogen bomb, which uses the more sophisticated process of nuclear fusion. The Indian government reported a number of successes after its rapid-fire series of tests in 1998, but press reports suggest that the scientists achieved less than they claimed.

Pakistan took a different route. It reportedly received some assistance from China in designing and testing its first nuclear device. While this may have speeded up the process of acquisition, Pakistani scientists have had to take many aspects of nuclear weapons design on faith. They lack the depth of understanding that comes from doing things on their own, a deficiency that will impede their progress toward more advanced weaponry in the future. India and Pakistan demonstrate that the barriers separating a country from nuclear capability are still high.

The third step in creating a nuclear weapon is making it robust enough to endure delivery by a missile or an aircraft. This is, let me assure you, no mean feat. Ballistic missiles are essentially controlled detonations in which the blast is directed out of a nozzle. A weapon mounted on the top of such a missile is subjected to intense vibrations that will shake apart anything not made to the most exacting engineering standards. Also, most long-range missiles fly into space before descending to their target. During reentry into the atmosphere the nose cone will glow white hot due to air friction. It is a major challenge to keep the weapon sufficiently cool that it will not explode in midflight. Add to this the problem of making a reliable electronic system to control the detonation of the device at the proper altitude and one can appreciate the challenges of "weaponizing" a design.

Miniaturization poses its own set of challenges. Press reports that terrorists might construct a "suitcase bomb"—one that could be easily carried to its target and left in a secret location for later detonation—are simply not credible. Only the United States and the Soviet Union have the capability to produce nuclear explosives that could be carried in a small suitcase, and even if those designs were known to a terrorist group, they would still need an impressive engineering capability to turn the blueprints into hardware.

I am sorry to say that on more than one occasion scaremongers from our nuclear weapons laboratories have attributed near superhuman status to other countries, giving them capabilities that even the United States would find challenging. This happened in 2004 when a Congressional commission looked at the threat posed by a high-altitude electromagnetic pulse (EMP). When a nuclear explosion occurs at an altitude above about 100,000 feet, the resulting radiation can produce an electromagnetic field, much like a radio pulse, directed downward. This pulse acts like electrical interference, and under just the right circumstances it can upset or even burn out delicate computers and other equipment. We've known about EMP for decades, from the time that a high-altitude nuclear test in the Pacific shut off some streetlights in Hawaii, but our increased dependence on high-tech gadgetry makes us more vulnerable than we have ever been before. EMP is something to be taken seriously. But there are limits to what can actually be achieved, and getting anywhere near to those limits requires all the sophistication—and nuclear test experience—that only an advanced nuclear nation can bring to bear.

One fast-talking scientist from the Lawrence Livermore National Laboratory convinced some members of Congress that North Korea could have such a device. (Fear always sells well on Capitol Hill.) I asked my associate, Jas Mercer-Smith, perhaps the most knowledgeable person in the world about such designs, for his opinion. Jas is a soft-spoken astrophysicist-turned-nuclear-weapons-designer. He has a boyish face that doesn't give away decades of all-nighters spent nursing complex calculations through the fastest computers of the day. He owns but a single shirt that is not white and long-sleeved, and he often quotes episodes from the early history of science to illustrate a complex point. Jas designed what is arguably the most sophisticated nuclear explosive ever tested by the United States, a device that pushed the limits of computational mathematics, physics, and our ability to measure things in the (to say the least) harshest radiation environments. "I don't think that the *United States* could do that sort of thing today," he told me. "To say that the North Koreans could do it, and without doing any testing, is simply ridiculous." Nevertheless, rumors are passed from one person to another, growing at every repetition, backed by flimsy or nonexistent intelligence and the reputations of those who are better at talking than doing. Jas was never asked for his opinion.

The good news is that even the best-financed and best-organized terrorist organization would be hard-pressed to take a stolen or purchased piece of special nuclear material and convert it into a workable nuclear weapon. In addition to the design and the materials, they would require machine shops, explosive testing ranges, sophisticated diagnostic equipment, and much more. The bad news is that, as the press seems to point out every day, more and more small countries are crossing the technological threshold that would permit them to make a weapon of their own. If an A. Q. Kahn had sold his drawings and parts to countries thirty years ago, they would have lacked the necessary infrastructure and skilled people to turn the ideas to reality. Today, many countries have those capabilities, and ready access to key ideas and hard-to-obtain parts could indeed enable them to enter the expanding nuclear club. For example, the computers that I used to design my first nuclear device were the most powerful in the world in the early 1980s, but they were much less capable than the laptop I currently use. Computer-controlled machine tools that were relatively rare a few decades ago can now be found in high-end auto repair shops.

Is the danger of terrorists getting a nuclear weapon overblown, something that we can ignore for the foreseeable future? Unfortunately not, since there is still the possibility that terrorists could buy, steal, or be given a device from an established nuclear power. Stealing a weapon is by far the most difficult path since, regardless of what is reported in the news, all nuclear nations take the security of their weapons very seriously. The Russian nuclear weapons laboratory at Arzamas-16 is protected by a triple array of fences nearly 20 feet tall that are regularly patrolled by guards and dogs and monitored by radar and other sensors. Could terrorists bribe a poorly paid Russian soldier to sell a weapon in a remote storage location? Maybe, but there would still be the problem of getting the weapon out of the country, a complex operation requiring planning and a knowledge of who needs to be bribed and when. Even if successful at stealing or buying a nuclear weapon, terrorists would need an expert to teach them how to operate the device. Unlike in the movies, a nuclear weapon does not have a red button on the side with an LED display that counts down the seconds to detonation. Most have complex interlocks designed to *prevent* unauthorized detonation; you would need the equipment and know-how to fool the weapon into thinking it was authorized to explode. And *very few* people have access to that equipment and know-how.

In 1997, Alexander Lebed, a retired Russian general and presidential hopeful, reported that a number of small nuclear weapons had gone missing from storage sites in that country. If true, it would have been a catastrophe waiting to happen. But it now appears that Lebed was merely reporting hearsay and speculating about what *might* have happened. In a country that kept almost everything secret, he was not on the list of people who had access to that type of information. And, even if he was right, he didn't address the problem of knowing how to detonate such weapons or the fact that most of those weapons were already well beyond their intended design lifetime. There was some question as to whether they would still work. As I have been told many times by high-ranking Russian officials, they have an even greater fear of "loose nukes" than we do since *they* are the ones surrounded by new countries with unstable governments, some of which have centuries-old grudges against Moscow. While there is an urgent need to improve the security at sites that store nuclear weapons and weapons-grade materials—something that Senators Nunn and Lugar have pushed with heroic determination—I believe that the Russians take their responsibilities seriously and I am aware of no credible evidence that a major theft has occurred.

It is more likely that an existing nuclear state would provide a terrorist with both a nuclear weapon and the technical expertise required to explode it. While this might appear the height of irresponsibility, a rogue element in the military of a developing nation might find it useful to have a nuclear-armed terrorist group that could make demands on the established government. There could be other scenarios, but the key point that I would like to make is that the more countries that have nuclear weapons, the greater the probability is that one of those weapons might go astray.

During the cold war, the United States developed a policy of deterrence that said that any nuclear attack against our country would be followed by a swift and overwhelming response. Other countries took this seriously, understanding that all that they held of value would be destroyed after a surprise attack on the United States. To-day, we face a different set of adversaries, terrorist groups and rogue states that either lack cities and industrial plants that can be threat-ened by nuclear weapons or those arrogant enough to test the resolve of the United States. The consequences of a nuclear explosion in a major metropolitan area are so extraordinary that we must pay atten-tion to any probability, no matter how small, that a determined ter-rorist group or rogue nation might gain access to a nuclear weapon.

However, there are limits to what even a nuclear explosion can do. As a rule of thumb, the death toll from a 10-kiloton weapon, the type that one might expect a lower-level nuclear state to develop, would be about 100,000 people. (For comparison, the atomic bomb dropped on Hiroshima had a yield of about 15 kilotons.) This is an extraordinary number, a tragedy of staggering proportions, but it is, in fact, comparable to the losses in the fire-bombing raids conducted during World War II, and it is less than would occur in some much less sophisticated attacks using chemicals or biological weapons.

Earlier, I presented two chilling scenarios, one involving a designer pathogen developed in a small biotechnology laboratory and the other involving the release of a large quantity of industrial chemi-cals. Whereas the development of a nuclear weapon would most likely require the resources of a nation-state, chemical and biological weapons can be produced by anyone with the necessary knowledge and skills.

That this isn't just alarmist speculation was graphically illustrated in the 2001 anthrax attack on the U.S. Senate. A staffer opening the mail in Senator Daschle's office would have attributed one letter to a fringe group except for the fine powder that fell out of the envelope along with the note. Upon analysis, the powder turned out to be a virulent form of anthrax, a form so pure and so fine that only an expert, someone who knew just about everything that there was to know about this type of biological weapon, could have made it. The Senate office building was evacuated and exposed personnel were quickly treated with powerful antibiotics. But, before the episode was over, several postal workers, who had been around letter-handling equipment through which the envelope had passed, were infected and died.

Who sent the anthrax? We don't know. Why did they send it? We don't know. Do they have more? We don't know. Was the anthrax produced in this country or was it imported from abroad? We don't know. After years of intensive investigation and an effort that involved the finest technical experts from around the world, the FBI still lacks definitive answers to these questions. Every test known to science was done to eke out any clue that might be left on the letter, the envelope, or the powder, but so far they have proved remarkably stubborn in giving up their secrets.

What we *do* know is that whoever did this was far more than an amateur who read about anthrax in a high school biology textbook and decided to make some as a prank. The anthrax used in the attack on the Senate required a great deal of skill and knowledge to produce. One leading expert in biological weapons told me that he did not think that he could produce anthrax of that quality in his laboratory. The challenge was more than just making the anthrax itself— the perpetrator had to know how to get it into the envelope without spreading it around so that other people would become sick, alerting the authorities. Maybe the perpetrator was willing to die for the cause, but it would certainly be noticed when a whole neighborhood came down with suspicious symptoms. This didn't happen and we still don't know where the material was made.

The equipment required to make anthrax is relatively easy to acquire; it is used in hundreds of biotechnology laboratories in universities and companies around the world. Studies have been done where a government agency created a front company just to see how difficult it would be to buy everything that would be required for a biological weapons capability. In no case did it take very long and in no case were they caught by suspicious authorities. There were just too many legitimate uses for the equipment and too many people using it to enable every single piece to be tracked. Nowadays it is knowledge and expertise rather than equipment that limits the production of biological weapons, and such knowledge and expertise is becoming more and more available with the globalization of science and technology. Even the seed stock that was used to start growing the anthrax used in the Senate attack was not difficult to obtain, since researchers sent small quantities of bacteria, including anthrax, through the regular mail, sometimes with no records kept of who received what. (Regulations did require record keeping for certain materials, but those regulations were sometimes ignored.) It takes only a minute amount of live bacteria to start a culture that could produce pounds of a biological weapon.

Anthrax is a naturally occurring bacterium found in cattle country and, once diagnosed, it is easy to treat with antibiotics available at any drugstore. With advancing capability in biotechnology, it will be possible for an attacker to modify the structure of anthrax at the microscopic level to make it much more resistant to any known treatment. In fact, multiple attacks could each use a slightly different form of the agent so that a different treatment would be needed every time, an all but hopeless task given the rapidity with which the disease acts.

There are even worse aspects to this problem. To be infected by anthrax, you have to be exposed to the original material. Other diseases, such as measles, smallpox, and influenza are passed from person to person, the human body effectively taking the role of a mobile manufacturing facility for the infection. Once one of these organisms enters the population, it can spread like wildfire, infecting hundreds or thousands of people before we are even aware that it exists. Since many pathogens have symptoms resembling common ailments like colds and flu, it would take time to realize that something out of the ordinary was happening. It could appear as just another naturally occurring epidemic. Only after several days would a patient's condition deteriorate to the point where it was clear that something more serious was afoot, and by that time it would be too late. True, physicians are now much more attentive to suspicious symptoms, but you only see a symptom after the infection has occurred, and a diagnosis can only be made if the person has the presence of mind, and the money, to go to a doctor.

This frightening scenario is no longer science fiction, since a research team recently announced that it had created, almost from scratch, a virulent organism just to show that it could be done. History tells us that what is challenging today will be old hat tomorrow, especially in such a fast-moving field as biotechnology. As more and more students learn the techniques of molecular manipulation in biological organisms, the possibility will only increase that one of them could use that knowledge to create a weapon rather than a cure.

While the equipment needed to make biological weapons is more readily available than the equipment needed to make a nuclear weapon, the material needed to conduct a large-scale chemical attack is all around us. Terrorists need not construct a laboratory to make a deadly nerve agent. Nor do they need to go to the trouble of stealing a chemical warhead from a storage facility in Russia, the United States, or elsewhere. One or two artillery shells loaded with a chemical agent might cause dozens of deaths, but nothing on the scale that could be achieved by using industrial chemicals already present in our own cities and neighborhoods.

Every year the industrial nations of the world produce thousands of tons of phosgene and chlorine, the very same chemicals that were used as poison gas weapons during World War I. While the Chemical Weapons Convention forbids making or stockpiling chemical weapons, countries are permitted to make these materials for legitimate industrial use. Phosgene, chlorine, and other noxious chemicals are employed for everything from water purification to semiconductor manufacturing and are transported in hundred-ton railcars through many of the major cities of the world. (Remember that the rail networks were originally intended to link the major metropolitan areas for freight and passenger service. There are few routes that don't pass through a major city.) Whereas a chemical attack during World War I used a few hundred pounds of lethal chemicals, a toxic release by terrorists could involve hundreds of *tons* of material, with a resulting death toll in the range of 100,000 to 300,000 people, more than would die from a low-yield nuclear explosion.

Am I giving ideas to the terrorists? Unfortunately not—they already know the destruction that would be caused by a massive chemical release. And they also know, if only by watching exposés on American television, that the security surrounding chemical plants and transportation facilities is woefully inadequate to protect us from such an attack. While the chemical and transportation industries are taking this problem seriously, progress has been slow, partly due to the challenge of improving security while maintaining industrial production and partly due to bureaucratic wrangling over the distribution of funds for homeland security.

A significant problem in dealing with the threat of weapons of mass destruction is getting the right level of realism in our planning. How should we deploy our resources to address the threats that we might face in the future? Should we invest more in maritime security to detect smuggled nuclear weapons or should we focus on tracking down dangerous materials abroad? Should we emphasize the nuclear threat or pay more attention to biological weapons? Mike Evenson, a senior manager at the Defense Threat Reduction Agency, was one of the first people to try to construct an overarching plan for defending the nation against nuclear and biological weapons, a plan that would actually make us safer rather than one based on a rush to "do anything as long as it looks like you're doing something." With his wiry build and thick Southern accent, Mike looks like he would be more at home on a tractor than in a Washington conference room, but he has a remarkable ability to see the big picture and make things happen.

When the country went on alert in the winter of 2001, fearing that terrorists had smuggled a nuclear weapon into a major city, there was a flurry of interest in high-tech radiation monitors, X-ray machines, and a myriad other as yet unproven gadgets that, for a king's ransom, could be put at airports, seaports, and border crossings. The scientific community was in overdrive, sensing lots of money for favored research projects, and the phrase "another Manhattan Project" was tossed about with reckless abandon.

Mike had a different idea. "What are we trying to do here? Supposin' we had all of this stuff right now. Would it catch somebody trying to get one of those things into the country?" Rather than start with the gadgets—which the scientists assured us would certainly solve *some* problem if we only poured enough money into them— Mike started with the threat. Where are the weapons and materials that we're worried about? Most of them are overseas, so start by working with other countries to make sure that their stores of weapons and weapons materials are safe and secure. Next, see about putting radiation and biological monitors at foreign seaports and airports. After all, you want to keep this stuff as far away from us as possible.

Then you can think about putting them at our points of entry and around key metropolitan areas and facilities. Finally, consider how you would respond to the consequences of an attack if, despite your best efforts, the attacker was successful. Using this "defense in depth" approach, Mike began the construction of a comprehensive plan that aimed to do as much as possible to protect the country while recognizing that no shield, no matter how sophisticated, would be leakproof. One need only look at the amount of illegal drugs that are smuggled into the country every day to see that.

With his rough Southern charm and a reputation for never taking no for an answer, Mike patrolled the corridors of the White House and the Pentagon, talking to whomever would listen. Progress was slow, particularly because of the furious turf battles that were going on at the time, battles waged by people who seemed more interested in how much control their offices had than actually getting anything done. "It's like pigs at the trough," Mike explained to me once after a particularly contentious meeting. "Half those people didn't have any idea what they wanted to do, but they sure as hell don't want *us* to do *anything*." But good ideas can occasionally win in even the most complex and bureaucratic of governments. Secretary of Homeland Security Tom Ridge was apparently given a copy of one of Mike's overarching plans and was so impressed that he ordered it implemented immediately, much to the chagrin of some of his staff. Mike's plan, which included everything from security upgrades in Siberia to protective gear in Peoria, became the start of a national effort to defend us against weapons of mass destruction. If the average American got to pick who they would rely on to defend the country, it would be someone like Mike Evenson.

The second threshold that we are crossing—the one related to the accelerating pace of events made possible by advances in communications and transportation—is no less important than the proliferation of weapons technology in determining our future. It is a truism that the pace of life only gets faster and faster. Two hundred years ago information moved at a human pace, limited by the speed of horse and sail. It took weeks for a letter to cross an ocean and even longer for one to cross a continent; there was a significant risk that it might never arrive at all. Travel between North America and Europe was a dreadful experience; even first-class passengers on a sailing ship endured endless days spent in cramped quarters, the victims of chronic seasickness. Prior to the invention of the telegraph and the undersea cable, wars raged for weeks or months after the opposing governments had agreed to cease hostilities; a treaty to end the War of 1812 was signed in Ghent in December 1814, but fighting continued until the spring of 1815, when news of the peace finally reached commanders in the field. Yet for all of these disadvantages, the speed of communications and transportation was very much in tune with a human timescale, a timescale that (often) enabled people to think about what was happening before events got out of hand. People wrote letters with pen and paper, and since those letters might take weeks to reach their destination there was a tendency to spend a bit more time on their contents than we spend on rapid-fire e-mails and text messages. There was, in short, a rough synchrony between the speed at which a person thought, the speed at which they composed their communications, and the speed with which those communications reached their intended destinations.

Paved roads, radio, and aircraft accelerated the pace of events, but the ability of decision makers to plot rational responses has remained the same. When the Germans invaded the USSR in World War II, Stalin refused to accept the intelligence reports and went into a several-day funk that no one dared to disturb. By the time he recovered, huge swaths of Soviet territory had been captured, along with massive quantities of vital Soviet military capability. General Douglas MacArthur demonstrated a similar inability to respond when he put off critical decisions for more than a day after the attack on Pearl Harbor, allowing the Japanese to destroy the few long-range bombers that could have helped delay the invasion of the Philippines. With one disaster following another, even the toughest of commanders can be worn down. Today, we face a nearly continuous series of crises, with no time to recover. Adding more bureaucrats won't help since the problem almost inevitably comes down to a single decision made at the top. To paraphrase the German rocket scientist Wernher von Braun, nine pregnant women will not produce a baby in one month. We are moving into a time when we need to plan and to engineer, to think ahead to how we would deal with even the least likely scenario to avoid being caught behind the proverbial eight ball when trouble strikes.

Today, we expect to be able to get any information that we want any time that we want it, from the latest on international events to the menu at the restaurant where we're having lunch. More than that, we expect to be able to reach anyone, anytime, anywhere with voice, text, and now even photographs. The development of telecommunications has taken us from a paucity of information to a glut of information, wanted and unwanted, that competes for our attention. When I was a student, a new research project involved days in the dusty stacks of the university library, a pocketful of change at the ready to pay for photocopies of useful articles. Now I do most of my searches online using electronic versions of hundreds of journals, some dating back over a century. I can find reams of information in an afternoon, and now one of my biggest problems is finding time to *read* everything that I find. Think about how telecommunications has changed your own life over just the past decade. How many online newspapers do you look at every day? How many websites are on your list of favorites, giving you information undreamed of ten years ago? On the other hand, how do you know that you can trust what you see on those websites?

The speed of communications is challenging us to make sense of the world; the proliferation of sources of information raises equal concern. No longer do people get their news mainly from newspapers, radio, and television, organizations that, for good or ill, controlled the flow of information to the public with at least a cursory interest in accuracy. People can now choose their own sources of information, sometimes going to places where truth is secondary to political motives or where only part of the story is told. Consider the following: During the 2003 invasion of Iraq, the Western press highlighted the extraordinary measures taken by American forces to minimize civilian losses, emphasizing that our troops were sometimes put at risk for fear of damaging a school or hospital. However, many television stations in the Arab world focused on the relatively few bombs and shells that went amiss and hit residential neighborhoods, giving the viewer the vivid impression that the Americans were intentionally targeting the civilian population to incite terror and panic. Both sides showed real footage, but the response of their audiences was predictably different.

Some people in the world still don't have enough information to understand what happened. Tanya Jandacek, a Peace Corps worker on the Pacific island of Kiribati, showed magazine photos of the September 11 attack on the World Trade Center to some of her neighbors. The daughter of artists and teachers, she grew up in the sheltered enclave of Los Alamos and after finishing university she decided to do something to help people less fortunate than herself. Tanya has the down-to-earth practicality of someone twice her age combined with a youthful determination to help. As she paged through the magazine photographs of New York, Washington, and Pennsylvania, she expected a reaction of sadness or perhaps even outrage, but her listeners seemed to brush it off. "We see that sort of thing all the time in movies about the United States," they replied. "It must be dangerous to live there." These people, intelligent in dealing with problems in their own world, lacked the information and experience required to understand events in another.

One of the reasons that the Communist parties of Eastern Bloc nations were able to remain in power so long is that they maintained a tight control on the media. During the cold war, it was against the law for people in those countries to listen to the Voice of America, the British Broadcasting Corporation, or other Western radio stations. Leaders kept their populations ignorant of the relative prosperity of capitalist nations and the fact that people could voice their opinions without fear of being arrested. Some violated the rules, and there was a brisk trade in forbidden literature, but the policy was generally successful and there was a feeling among even the best-educated people that they lived about as well as anyone else in the world. I remember Olga Tatsenko, one of the first Russian weapons scientists to come to Los Alamos as part of our collaborative program, being stopped at U.S. Customs because she was carrying a suitcase full of bread and sausages. Her explanation was simple: "How could we expect you to feed all five of us for two weeks? Where would you find the extra food?" Surely one of the reasons for the breakup of the Soviet Union was the realization that it was no longer possible to keep the lid on news from abroad, that the people would find out that they did not, in fact, live as well as many other people in the world, and that there was a clear correlation between their standard of living and the policies of their government.

Today, you don't have to be a news organization to affect the opinions of millions. A single person with a computer and a website can reach a huge number of people in the time it takes to type a message, scan a photograph, or upload a video clip. Individuals can spread their opinion around the world faster than responsible governments can think of a response, inflaming passions that are often remarkably resistant to later correction. Governments are left in the unenviable mode of playing catch-up, responding to what has already happened, knowing that opinions, once set, can be remarkably resistant to change. This happened in 2006 after cartoons depicting the prophet Mohammed in a Danish newspaper sparked riots throughout the Middle East. By the time that Western governments were aware of the problem, it was out of control.

Information is reaching a far broader audience than ever before. As recently as thirty years ago, the average rural citizen of India and China lived in relative isolation, knowing only his or her own village, the next village, and a little bit about the outside world. Barring wars and taxes, you were pretty much on your own, a situation summarized marvelously well by the Russian saying, "God is in heaven and the tsar is in Moscow." Today, many of even the most remote villages have satellite television and cell phones, giving people at least the opportunity to gain an accurate perception of their place in the world. Rural populations everywhere are growing impatient for improvements to their way of life, improvements that they now know are possible, and this impatience is beginning to influence the ballot box. Beijing understands that it can no longer focus only on the big cities. It knows that it has to pay more attention to the hundreds of millions of impoverished peasants in the countryside. The information revolution has already spread well beyond the developed nations, or even the major cities of the developing countries. It is affecting everyone, everywhere.

Advances in transportation have changed our lives in equally profound ways. More people than ever are visiting other parts of the world, giving them a better appreciation of other cultures. Less and less can one use the old joke, "To Americans, foreign news is what happens to Americans while they are abroad." Today it's cheaper to buy a discount ticket from New York to London than it is to buy a regular coach ticket from New York to Cleveland. We are frustrated when it takes more than one day to ship our business package from Washington to Tokyo or when we have to get a visa to visit another country. If the local shop is out of our favorite French cheese, our immediate reaction is to go to the Internet to find a way to have it shipped directly to our home from Paris. We are growing used to living in a global village.

However, these improvements in global transportation bring their own set of challenges. Only a few percent of the cargo containers coming into this country receive even the most cursory inspection. For the rest, the government relies on the shipper's manifest as sufficient evidence of what they carry. While airline passengers are tightly screened, sometimes to the point of absurdity, scant attention is paid to the tons of cargo carried below the passenger's feet, cargo that could include a tiny quantity of a biological weapon hidden amid a thousand vials of legitimate medication. Is that modeling clay or high explosive, a DVD player or a detonator? Simply put, we haven't a clue what is crossing our borders every day, and keeping track of the sheer volume of international travel and transport is a challenge that will only increase.

We are crossing a fundamental threshold with communications and transportation technology: things are now happening faster than a human being can think about them. Military planners describe this as "being inside the decision loop of the enemy"—acting faster than one's opponent can understand and react to what is happening. In the Iraq war of 2003, the Iraqi command and control structure was so slow that by the time Saddam Hussein heard of an American advance it was already too late for him to respond. He couldn't predict where we would strike next and he couldn't act fast enough to reinforce his troops once an attack occurred. The same thing can happen in the business world when a successful company is able to marshal information faster than its opponents, controlling rather than responding to market conditions.

However fast our communications, however vast the amount of information at our fingertips, human beings think on a *human* timescale, one that is built into our brain and one that is unlikely to change anytime soon. Consider the last time that someone close to you died or was involved in an automobile accident. How long did it take before you were able to think and act normally, to plan for the future rather than be totally focused on that one event? If you are like most people, it took you about eight to twelve hours to recover some perspective, to get beyond the initial shock and determine what to do next. "OK, the car is gone, but we can get another one. The good news is that no one was injured. In the meantime, I need to get a rental car and get started on the insurance paperwork." You went over and over the event in your mind, called up family and friends to talk about it, all the while attempting to make sense of what happened. It takes a period of time to integrate something radical into our overall pattern of remembered experience, a period of time that has not changed at anywhere near the pace of the events affecting us. It is certainly true that some people can keep their cool in almost any circumstance, and training can improve our ability to respond to dangerous situations, but we can still only handle so much information at so rapid a rate. The problem is that there is too much information and material in motion, some of which could have a big impact on our lives. And don't think that government officials are any different in this respect than you are. They have their own challenges in keeping up with events and planning for the future. This is a problem affecting everyone.

Combining these advances in communications and transportation with the growing ability of small groups to cause mass destruction makes for an especially deadly cocktail. As recently as two decades ago, only a few countries could threaten serious damage to the United States and they had value systems much like our own. We expected to be able to see trouble far enough in advance that we could make appropriate preparations. Today we face a larger number of potential adversaries, including well-funded extremist groups, who can act with lightning speed. We no longer have the luxury of responding to events—we have to *anticipate* the types of things that can happen and shape our actions to maximize the probability of good futures and minimize the probability of bad ones. You might say that this is too hard, that there are too many variables, too many people involved. It's a utopian idea that won't work in the real world. Well, what's the alternative—to carry on as we are, to muddle through whatever fate throws our way, to hope for the best? That didn't work very well a century ago, when it took months to assemble an army for an invasion, and it certainly won't work in a future where a determined adversary can destroy that army before it leaves home using weapons of mass destruction. We face a future in which the opinion of hundreds of millions of people can be turned against us by a few zealots who know how to use communications technology to their advantage. It's a new game with new rules, and we had best learn to play it well.

|| **how culture and ecology will limit our actions**

That nature still defeats
The frowsty science of the cloistered men,
Their theory, their conceits . . .
—VITA SACKVILLE-WEST

Every now and again we are reminded that, despite all our technological prowess, we are not the supreme rulers of the earth. This les-
son came home to me in a very personal way when a forest fire nearly
destroyed my town in May 2000. On an otherwise typical Thursday
afternoon, the National Park Service decided to set a controlled burn
near the Bandelier National Monument, quite close to the town and
laboratory of Los Alamos. One can question the wisdom of setting a
fire at that particular time—it was the driest spring in decades and
there was a strong wind blowing—but they felt that it was important
to clear away dry underbrush that could provide fuel to a fire started
by careless campers or lightning. This is done quite often in this part
of the country and for two days things seemed to be going according
to plan.

However, the very dry conditions, strong winds, and proximity of Bandelier to Los Alamos made many local residents increasingly uneasy over the following days. On Sunday afternoon I decided to check on things. As my car rounded a curve where there was a clear view, I was shocked to see a massive column of dirty brown smoke rising from the mountains behind the laboratory—ironically, a column that looked like a nuclear mushroom cloud. Apparently the Park Service had waited too long to call for help in containing their controlled burn, and the result was a rampaging fire that was advancing across thousands of acres of pristine national forest. I watched individual sap-rich trees burst into columns of flame hundreds of feet tall, a death flare that lasted only a few seconds before it was passed along to the next tree.

There was great sadness among the few people who were permitted to be that close to the fire, a sadness that will be familiar to anyone who lives in a beautiful part of the world threatened by the forces of nature. Those lovely green mountains that one could so easily imagine to be inhabited by the sacred spirits of the Native Americans were being destroyed. It was more than the loss of scenery; this was a living, spiritual place, with elk and deer and bear—a forest that had taken centuries to grow and that would take centuries to replace.

A few days later, my drive to the lab revealed flames on both sides of the road; the smoke was so thick that you could hardly see over the hood of the car. There was a feeling of being alone against a titanic and impersonal force of nature—not a feeling of fear but of powerlessness against something primal, something that was defeating all of our sophisticated theories and conceits. By that time, thousands of people were fighting the fire on the ground and in the air. We talked about the fire as if it were a cunning beast with a mind of its own.

When it was all over, 400 homes had been destroyed and over 47,000 acres were turned from beautiful mountain forest into grotesque black sticks. To a town with the highest concentration of Ph.D.s on the planet, one known for creating the most destructive weapons in history, it was a slap in the face, a reminder that all of our knowledge was useless to protect us from the same nature that we were so proud of controlling. For months after the fire, we drove through a horrific landscape of destruction, our arrogance taken down several pegs. I remember a Washington official casually re-marking, "Fire's out—you guys need to get back to work." He didn't understand. It wasn't only the tangible losses that continued to hurt, but the feeling that the spirits who lived in those mountains had de-serted us.

Everyone is fascinated by photos of Earth taken from space, the ones that show a beautiful blue sphere clothed in brilliant white clouds, an island home floating in a sea of darkness. One reason for this fascina-tion is that it lets us see ourselves in perspective—where we are and even what we are—so it's understandable that the arrival of these stunning photographs was accompanied by a heightened concern for what we are doing to our environment, the fragile ecosystem that gives us the air we breathe, the water we drink, and the food we eat. Standing on the ground, it is easy to get the impression that the world is vast, almost limitless, and that it can withstand even the most de-termined human assaults. But when we see it from a distance, when we appreciate in our gut as well as our brain that it is finite and, at least for the time being, inescapable, then we quite naturally become concerned about what is happening to it.

Human-induced changes in the environment didn't begin with rampant industrialization and urban sprawl. We have shown our-selves quite capable of effecting drastic changes in our landscape even without advanced technology. As Jared Diamond points out in his book *Guns, Germs, and Steel,* when the Maori arrived in New Zealand about a thousand years ago they found a land rich in plant and animal life, including a sizable population of large mammals. Within a few hundred years, the Maori hunted those large animals to extinction—they killed every last one of them. Similarly, Easter Island used to be covered with thick forests that provided food, medicine, and a habitat for a small animal population. In the process of building dozens of huge stone heads and ceremonial altars, the Easter Islanders cut down every one of the trees on the island, leaving nothing that could regenerate the original ecosystem. Because of the isolation of these islands, decisions made centuries ago affect people today: the results were permanent. Modern cultures have proved equally capable of causing irreparable damage to the environment. There are places in Russia where so much toxic material was dumped on the ground that *cubic kilometers* of dirt are contaminated. Even the scope of the problem is uncertain, because in Soviet days the plant managers didn't bother to keep records of how much waste was dumped where. The Aral Sea is a fraction of its former size as a result of water being diverted for grand agricultural projects. And the area around the Chernobyl nuclear power plant will be unsuitable for human habitation for decades, or even centuries. In the United States, several towns have been evacuated due to industrial pollution.

Sometimes we *are* smart enough to realize what we're doing and make the necessary changes to avert further damage. For example, at the end of the nineteenth century a combination of natural climatic conditions and the burning of coal as a fuel was causing "pea soupers"—London fogs so thick that traffic moved at a slow crawl. People were beginning to suffer serious respiratory problems. The city council enacted legislation to reduce the use of sooty fuels, and within a few years air quality improved dramatically. A similar thing happened in the United States in the 1970s when smog from automobiles, power plants, and factories began to cause health problems in major cities. We changed laws, invented new technologies, and changed our driving habits to reduce a manifestly serious threat to our well-being. As intelligent beings, if we see a problem develop we can take measures to prevent it, a promising attribute when one thinks of the risks that we face from weapons of mass destruction. We really *can* change if we want to.

The elimination of large animals in New Zealand and the unhealthy fogs of London were serious problems, but at least they were relatively local in effect. Today we face a new set of *global* environmental challenges, challenges that will have as profound an influence on our future as any government decision or new technology. For one thing, it now appears certain that the average temperature of our planet is increasing and that this global warming will impact everything from crop yields to the value of beachfront real estate. While most scientists think that global warming is linked to human production of carbon dioxide, others point out that temperature fluctuations have happened before and that, sooner or later, the planet should cool off again. But no matter what the cause, it seems clear that over the next few decades coastal regions will suffer from a rise in sea levels caused by the melting of the polar ice caps. Northern latitudes will benefit from warmer temperatures and improved agricultural productivity associated with a longer growing season. Unfortunately, as the tsunami of 2004 illustrated, many of the poorest countries face the sea, so the effect of global warming will be to make the poorer nations even poorer and the richer northern countries even richer. This widening of the income gap among rich and poor countries will only exacerbate global tensions, especially since most of the blame for the changes will fall upon the industrialized countries that produce most of the world's greenhouse gases. While it seems unlikely that countries will go to war over environmental issues, increased concern will certainly complicate international affairs and could contribute to violence.

A second problem that we need to face up to is the dwindling supplies of cheap natural resources. A century ago, the earth seemed to offer a limitless supply of almost everything that we needed and most of it was within relatively easy reach. Today, oil reserves are dwindling as our appetite for energy continues to increase. The deposits of the North Sea are already beginning to give out and the same thing will ultimately happen in oil-rich Middle Eastern countries. Even if we continue to locate new reserves of oil, they may be in remote places or in a form that is more expensive to extract and process. Natural resources will play an even more important role in future international affairs as countries used to easy cash based on oil exports scramble to develop other means to feed, house, and employ their people. If you are worried about fundamentalist Islamic groups in Saudi Arabia today, think about what will happen when the oil gives out and there is insufficient money to give every citizen a handout and where having a job is a necessity rather than a desirable way to spend one's time. Think about how Africa might look if countries had to find means of income other than natural resources—a continent already scarred by war and disease may well stand at the brink of an even greater catastrophe. Access to natural resources was a principal reason for Japanese expansion in World War II. Recent foreign incursions into the Congo were done as much for diamonds as to help quell that country's disastrous civil war.

While we could learn to live with less oil or diamonds, we cannot live without adequate supplies of clean water and we are beginning to touch upon the limits of underground aquifers and even major rivers. With the world's population expected to top 9 billion by 2050, there is serious concern over where we will get the water for all these people. Relatively new technologies, such as desalinization of seawater, could work but only at a much higher cost than we pay today, affecting our ability to buy things and contribute to economic development around the world. Access to water could very well create a new class of haves and have-nots and a new set of domestic and international tensions. And the pressure will be even greater than it is for oil. Whereas oil is a necessity for industrial society, water is absolutely essential to all life.

Finally, we need to understand that nature is itself dynamic; it can and does produce its own surprises. The influenza epidemic of 1918 killed more people than the First World War. Could the flu, which for most people is more of an annoyance than a life-threatening disease, once again mutate to resist our most powerful treatment? Or could some other exotic disease jump from an animal species to humans, adapting to its new host and causing unprecedented carnage before we could develop a cure? The AIDS virus, which has existed for only about half a century, now threatens to fundamentally change the demographics of Africa as it kills tens of millions of men and women in the most productive phase of their lives. Humankind faces risks of new diseases that could arise as a result of the very medical treatments that we use to cure old ones. Antibiotics might kill 99.9 percent of a germ, but that remaining 0.1 percent could survive and adapt to become an even greater threat. Nature can exact its own revenge on those who despoil it.

Equally important to the physical environment in human affairs is the impact of *cultures*, those systems of rules, beliefs, traditions, and artifacts that structure our individual and social lives. We like to think of ourselves as independent people, able and even insistent about deciding what we do and with whom we associate. However, much of our behavior is shaped by the culture in which we live, and for good reason. Think about how difficult your day would be if you had to make a conscious decision about every minor action that you took. Why do you stop at traffic lights when your car is the only one on the street and there are no police around to give you a ticket? Why do you hold the door for someone when it would be easier and faster for you to enter first? What causes us to line up in an orderly fashion at the movie theater instead of pushing and shoving to get to the front? Much of our behavior is automatic, based on a learned system of customs that makes social life possible and which frees us from the otherwise incredible burden of having to think about each and every action that we take throughout our day. We act in certain ways with the expectation that others will do likewise and, in so doing, we prevent social chaos. Abiding by a common set of rules, we are able to focus our energy and attention on more important things.

But society is more than a collection of individuals following the same set of cultural rules. To further simplify how we interact with the billions of other people in the world, we have granted groups and organizations identities of their own, ranging from the nuclear family to the multinational corporation. We talk about the "Jones family" even though it is in fact a collection of individuals; we talk about the "Islamic street" as if all Muslims believe exactly the same thing and act in exactly the same say. We have created a whole spectrum of groups from families to cities to nations. We are Joneses, Bostonians, and Americans all at the same time. Councils of mayors help coordinate the activities and policies of neighboring cities. International diplomacy helps regulate interactions on a global scale. At each level of society, there are sets of accepted standards of value and behavior—a culture—that help bring order to what would otherwise be anarchy.

Culture is more than desirable; it is essential in helping us satisfy our strong need for companionship. In the early twentieth century, British doctors worried about orphaned infants being exposed to unnecessary germs and thought that minimizing their contact with caregivers would reduce the incidence of illness. But exactly the opposite happened: mortality rates of almost 100 percent occurred among babies deprived of human contact. A similar effect has been observed in monkeys, where, given an option, a baby will choose a stuffed image of its mother over food. Companionship is more than a want; it is a need as critical to human beings as food and water, a need that must be met to maintain sanity and life itself. We join clubs, work in teams, and strike up conversations with total strangers just for the pleasure of having contact with other people. We enjoy things more when we share them with others even when that sharing comes at a cost to ourselves. We are a social species.

All of this would be well and good if everyone agreed on the same set of cultural norms, the same set of good and bad behaviors that should be followed. Unfortunately, after a century of searching, sociologists and anthropologists have been unable to agree on almost any set of universal or natural human values. Even some of the most basic behaviors differ among societies. For example, while most cultures condemn incest, the ancient Egyptians and Hawaiians encouraged marriage between royal siblings as a means to maintain a pure bloodline, essential for the continuance of political order. Marriages between first cousins were common among the royal families of Europe for the same reason, and more than one birth defect resulted from the practice. Most societies defend the right of private property, but many egalitarian societies have existed for thousands or tens of thousands of years with no concept of private ownership. Material goods belong to everyone and it would be considered the height of incivility to refuse something after a polite request. Even in modern society, we treat some property as "common," including public lands and equipment belonging to a health or sporting club to which we belong. A prohibition against murder is another apparently "natural" law of human behavior, but state-sponsored executions are still practiced in some countries and terrorists deem the taking of innocent lives an acceptable means of achieving their political ends. As previously mentioned, it was legal to kill someone in Afghanistan if it was done in a fair fight, and in many countries revenge killings are still viewed as having a certain justification.

Business and diplomacy can be complicated when the two sides come from different cultures, something that I experienced when I was negotiating the first agreements between the nuclear weapons laboratories of the United States and Russia. As we were coming to closure on a program of joint experiments, I mentioned that, while I was happy with the agreement, I would have to get the approval of our contracting person to make it official. "Aha!" said Valarie, my Russian counterpart, "We've been talking to the wrong person! We should be talking to the contract man who has the authority." I patiently explained that I had the final decision, but that the contract officer knew the right legal terminology to make the agreement binding. After further discussion, I realized that we were approaching things from fundamentally different perspectives: as an American, I lived in a *law-based* culture, where it was assumed that everyone, no matter how powerful, followed the same rules. Valarie was part of a *power-based* culture, where the boss decided the best course of action and the underlings fit the rules to that decision. In later negotiations, I found that the notion of a "level playing field" was literally a foreign concept to many Russians. The whole point of a negotiation, they thought, was to get as much as possible in exchange for as little as possible. It's not that they were greedy; it was just how they saw the world. What was pushy for us was perfectly acceptable for them.

One can posit a third type of culture, an *honor-based* system in which the reputation of the individual is of greater value than either law or power. Much of the Islamic world is honor-based. One might be poor and lowly placed, but to have one's honor makes one a man, a notion wonderfully expressed by the Iraqi saying "I am a man with a mustache," that is, a grown man. Interactions between our material and law-based culture and an honor-based culture can be just as complex as between Russia and the United States, as I found once when a representative of the U.S. Army asked me how much money it would take to get an Afghan warlord to turn over members of Al Qaeda. "None," was my answer, since the idea of sacrificing loyalty for money would be so abhorrent to those tribesmen that we would only attract the worst of the lot, those who would turn on us as quickly as they turned on their former allies. To win loyalty, one must first win respect, something that takes time. This is difficult for Americans to understand because they live in a culture of instant gratification.

Lacking consensus on the most basic human values, could one hope to construct a set of behavioral norms that optimizes the positive aspects of human behavior while minimizing the worst of our excesses? There was a time when it was hoped that we could do just that. Philosophers such as John Locke, Jean-Jacques Rousseau, and Baruch Spinoza proposed that the scientific method, applied so successfully to the physical world, might be just as applicable to the social world. Spinoza went so far as to construct a logical theory of ethics using geometric proofs, hoping to provide a complete and consistent system of behavior based on fundamental axioms agreeable to everyone. The idea was that once people saw the logic of the whole scheme, they would naturally want to adapt their behavior and reap the benefits. John Locke thought social progress primarily a matter of educating the young in the proper rules of behavior and isolating them from the corrupting influences of the world; within a generation, or two or three, he reasoned, the world would right itself and everyone would live happily ever after—an early form of the "end of history" argument. Rousseau wrote of a social contract between government and the population that spelled out the expectations on each side, a means of eliminating misunderstandings that could lead to violence. Numerous communities were started to implement "scientific" schemes for society, little utopias that bravely experimented with communal living and rational means of governance, but all of them failed for one reason or another, most frequently because of internal dissension that led to disillusionment and social disintegration.

Books on culture change are a staple in business literature, but the very fact that there are so many of them suggests that this is a *really hard problem*, even in a well-structured and disciplined corporation where, at least nominally, the boss has the final say. We're used to acting in certain ways and changing those ways makes us uneasy, unsure of our future place in the world. People stay in unsatisfying jobs because they are afraid of risking a stable situation for the unknown. Organizations resist change because of the vested interests of their participants and because it is difficult to get a large number of people to agree on almost any course of action. Revolutions happen when frustration rises to the boiling point and people remove power from the government in favor of a different system.

But if cultural values are so difficult to change, are we really tilting at windmills when we hope to reduce the threat of mass violence by modifications in our social and political institutions? Are we locked into a set of cultural patterns from which there is no escape, or escape only after many generations of effort? No, and there are some success stories that can inspire us to believe that we really can cause fundamental change, and do it quickly.

Many people have heard at least parts of President John Kennedy's 1961 speech where he announced his intention to "send a man to the Moon and return him safely to the Earth." Fewer people know *why* President Kennedy chose to spend so much of the nation's treasure on what was, despite the many scientific and technological spinoffs of the space program, essentially a stunt. In the late 1950s, American leaders were concerned that, contrary to all expectations, Soviet communism seemed to be working very well. Lenin's dream of world socialism might actually happen. The Soviets were training legions of talented scientists and engineers, a fact shockingly demonstrated by their launch of the first artificial satellite, while American students majored in liberal arts and business, thinking of scientists (and most other intellectuals) as "eggheads." Kennedy knew that he needed to change American opinion about science and he needed to do it fast. And he knew that success required more than the invention of another government program, putting more money into science education, or giving bigger contracts to defense contractors—he had to get the *whole population* behind an idea that would make people want to learn about science. Over the course of several months, the White House looked at various ways to get the interest of the general public; maybe we could drill down into the earth, explore the oceans, or unlock the mysteries of the human body. Finally, with no small amount of pressure from the aerospace industry, the decision was made to focus on space, something that was exciting and understandable to the average person, yet something that would require a massive shift in educational patterns. For added emphasis, Kennedy decided to send human beings into space. In this, he went against the advice of his top scientists, who correctly argued that satellites could collect scientific data perfectly well without people tending them and that a massive life-support system would only detract from the amount of instrumentation that could be carried aloft. But Kennedy understood that the presence of a man would rivet the attention of every American on every phase of the program. Watching space launches was the one and only time that a television was permitted into my elementary school classroom. If it weren't for the roar of the rocket, you could have heard a pin drop when John Glenn was launched into orbit. Some of my friends sent their weekly allowance to NASA to help speed us to the moon. Science and engineering went from uncool to cool, the place for bright kids to be. So when people ask whether the Apollo program was worth the cost, we can answer that it was a bargain: never before has such far-reaching social change been accomplished so quickly at so small an investment.

As Eric Hoffer wrote in his insightful book *The True Believer*, real change requires two things: a frustrated population looking for change and a leader who can take that population to a new place. In the 1950s and 1960s, Americans were worried about the Soviet Union, with its huge rockets and massive army. Kennedy knew that the United States had to change and he offered a vision of a future that excited everyone. Contrast the race to the moon with other programs that might have been equally valuable, such as President Reagan's Strategic Defense Initiative, which tried to construct an impenetrable shield against Russian missiles. The stimulus—fear of Soviet aggression—was the same one that Kennedy faced, but the character of the proposal was fundamentally different. At the time, I was the leader of the group designing the nuclear explosive–driven X-ray laser, a device that Edward Teller (incorrectly) told Reagan was ready to enter the engineering phase for deployment into space. This was a huge scientific undertaking that made incredible progress, but even so it lacked the excitement of Neil Armstrong's first steps on the moon or even the Hubble telescope's first photos of the deepest reaches of space. Kennedy proposed something constructive, something that appealed to our natural instinct for exploration. Reagan wanted to *prevent* something from happening, quite a different psychological motivation. Kennedy started a program that was visible to everyone, while Reagan's program was shrouded in secrecy. It *is* possible to change, but only if the population is ready for change and if leadership has a positive idea for the future.

This is precisely our task: to create a vision of the future that will excite people and make them want change in ways that will reduce the possibility of mass violence. We can't just focus on the bad stuff—horror stories of what might happen. Preaching at one another has failed in the past and, I believe, it will fail in the future. We must offer a constructive and creative vision of a future that we can move *toward*, rather than one that we wish to *escape*. In a sense, humanity is growing up, moving beyond the time when it can happily focus on today and into a period when it needs to think about the consequences of its actions on a global scale.

|| **why most strategic plans fail**

There is always an easy solution to every
human problem—neat, plausible, and
wrong.   —H. L. MENCKEN

Being in the nuclear weapons business does not always endear one to
university audiences. Recently I gave a talk entitled "A University's
Role in the Fight Against World Terrorism," in which I argued that
our country needed fresh ideas to help us solve what is really an incredibly difficult problem. Since ideas are the lifeblood of universities, it seemed to me only natural that we should engage the academic
community in a productive way. How can we better understand why
people choose violence as a means to achieve their ends and how can
we convince them to stop?

After my talk I found that some of my listeners were suspicious of
having anything to do with national security. They were concerned
about being conscripted by the CIA and the Pentagon, losing their
academic freedom, and trading intellectual integrity for research
funding. These are certainly serious issues, especially for scholars
who have invested a lifetime in pursuit of the truth. But I strongly
believe that only by engaging the best minds across the widest spectrum of disciplines can we optimize our chances for success. Living

in society brings with it certain responsibilities, including the responsibility to help prevent evil. There are many ways to help, from dedicated pacifism to the use of force.

I have always had the greatest respect for true pacifists, people who object to the very notion of violence and refuse to participate in violent acts no matter what the provocation. People like Mahatma Gandhi, Martin Luther King Jr., and others have shown the incredible power of peaceful convictions, changing the apparently unchangeable without the use of force. To patiently and persistently work for what is right, knowing full well the dangers of acting from a position of weakness, seems to me the pinnacle of heroism. However, while Gandhi and King largely achieved their goals of independence for India and greater equality for people of color, others were less fortunate. When the great German theologian Deitrich Bonhoffer spoke out against the Nazis, they simply sent him to a concentration camp and later executed him. We will never know the names of the many who tried to do good in the face of manifest evil and perished in the attempt.

King once said that peaceful resistance was effective because oppressors didn't know how to deal with nonviolent people. When a riot occurs, it is easy to justify the use of force to maintain public order, but when people merely refuse to go along with injustice, it is much harder to justify a harsh response. However, such a philosophy works only when the larger society has a developed moral conscience; it fails miserably when the larger society doesn't care or actively supports the suppression of the protesting group. Nonviolent resistance didn't work in the Soviet Union when revolutionary zeal, combined with an interlocking system of surveillance and fear, led to the imprisonment and death of over 20 million Russians, most of whom were *believers* in the cause. And nonviolent resistance fails when the perpetrators of the violence never see their intended victims, as when a population is bombed from high altitude or attacked with ballistic missiles.

There is no question that violence is a bad thing. But is it *always* wrong? Are there situations where a violent act might be justified in order to prevent something worse? Everyone knows the types of moral dilemma that are used in discussions of situational ethics, ones that asked whether you would use force to protect yourself, your family, a friend, or even a stranger. Here's a slightly different scenario that is more relevant to our discussion about reducing the threat of mass violence.

Suppose you are in a room with one other person. That person is physically bigger and stronger than you and is assembling a large bomb, a bomb that could kill hundreds of people if detonated. You try to convince him to stop, emphasizing the number of innocent people who will suffer, but he merely shrugs and continues with his work. You try to pull him away from the bomb, to keep him from connecting the final wires, without success. Finally, you realize that nothing that you say is going to dissuade the man from killing you and many more people in the building. What would you do? Would you stand by your nonviolent principles and let him proceed, maybe hoping that he would see the light at the last second? Would you pick up a hammer and hit him on the head, hoping to knock him out long enough to call for help? If the hammer was a knife, would you stab him, perhaps even kill him, trading his life for hundreds of others? Part of the heroism of the true pacifist is being willing to die or watch others die rather than commit a violent act. No sacrifice, they argue, is worth crossing the line to do the very thing that they object to in others. The problem in this particular example is that your decision has consequences well beyond yourself—your failure to take positive action will result in the deaths of many innocent people. Like most really difficult problems, there is no perfect solution. Moralists have argued for centuries about what constitutes a just cause for using violence, be it violence against an individual or a preemptive war against a nation. The hardest decisions to make are the ones with no clear answers.

One thing that I have learned from working in government is that it is always easier to deal with a difficult question when you know that you are not responsible for the answer. Critics can hold forth on what they think needs to be done, and often quite sincerely, but they are never held to account by consequences. People in government don't have that luxury and must live with the real-world result of every decision they make. Would it have been better for the United States to have stayed out of World War II, giving Japan what it wanted and allowing the Nazis to complete the extermination of millions more Europeans? Or, should we have jumped into the fight earlier, perhaps even preemptively attacking Germany before the Nazi war machine had the chance to reach its full potential? Would we then have been accused of giving up on Neville Chamberlain's diplomacy before it had a chance to bear fruit? These aren't hypothetical questions but very real ones that President Franklin Roosevelt and his cabinet struggled with for months before the attack on Pearl Harbor made the issue a moot point. In a more modern example, while we now know that there were no weapons of mass destruction in Iraq, that they had been destroyed years before, at the time that President Bush made the decision to invade, the intelligence community told him that the threat was very real. History will judge the efficacy of invading Iraq, but the decision was made by people who thought that they were taking the least harmful course for the long term.

As difficult as these decisions were, we are about to face a whole new set of challenges that promise to confound even the wisest of leaders. Whereas in the past we could react to events as they un-folded—declaring war after we were attacked and preempting a ca-pability to launch weapons of mass destruction—in the future things will happen so fast, and could have such devastating consequences, that we will need to think about what we'll do *before* the problem be-comes acute. And since the consequences of an event involving a weapon of mass destruction could easily spill over national borders, this planning is going to have to occur on the global level. For the first time in our history, we need to start thinking of ourselves as more than New Yorkers, or Americans, or Westerners but as *homo sa-piens*. We need to start thinking at the species level.

There are two parts to planning—knowing where you want to go and figuring out how to get there. They are linked, since it would be foolish to commit to a goal that had little or no chance of being real-ized. For example, if our goal was the elimination of *all* violence, then we might choose to put everyone on a strong tranquilizer drug. Un-realistic you might say, and you would be right, but would it be any more realistic to insist that all of the world's totalitarian governments immediately stop oppressing their people, grant real democracy, and set up a free-market economy? Goals and planning go hand in hand, each influencing the other.

Our goal in this book is to identify practical measures to reduce the probability of mass violence. I have kept this general, using "re-duce" rather than "reduce by 80 percent" or some other quantitative measure. The reason is, quite honestly, that *any* reduction from what we had in the last bloody century would be a plus, giving hundreds of thousands of people the opportunity to live and contribute to the world's society.

What are the specific steps that we can take, what are the practical, achievable objectives that can be written down and presented to the people and the governments of the world? What are steps one, two, and three? How much will it cost and who will do it? Why do we think that this approach will work when so many other efforts have failed? These questions will be addressed in the remainder of this book. Yes, it's hard and many have tried before, but the problem of mass violence is so real and so threatening that *not to try* would be to accept the almost historical guarantee that there will be more and greater suffering in the future.

Large-scale social planning has proved easier said than done. All governments have plans for their annual budgets, and many have multiyear plans to manage big projects. Under communism the Soviet Union and China prepared elaborate five-year plans that were designed to usher in world socialism, each announced with great fanfare. Unfortunately, even the most detailed plans often foundered upon the rocks of unforeseen events, lack of cooperation by the population, and wishful thinking. Even some scholarly planning studies that tried to incorporate the best information available failed miserably to predict the future. A couple of examples will help to illustrate how we've gone wrong.

Thomas Robert Malthus was an English clergyman with an interest in demographics. Born in 1766 in Guilford, Surrey, Malthus was for many years a fellow at Cambridge University. He lived and worked during the Enlightenment, a time when leading thinkers were convinced that rational thought and the purposeful design of improved social institutions could lead to the betterment of all humanity. After all, hadn't rational thought led to the astonishing advances in science that were transforming life through the steam engine, the powered loom, and other marvels of industrialization? So enthusiastic were philosophers that they believed that human beings could be "perfected" if only they could find and implement the right social institutions. One had only to think carefully about the desired goals, decide on the right methods to achieve them, and all would be well.

Malthus spent endless hours debating these issues, struck by the stark contrast between the rosy predictions of the philosophers and the dismal conditions in which the vast majority of the English population lived. This was the time of migration from the countryside to industrial cities, when people were surviving ten to a room with barely enough food to live, a time when a growing social conscience and rising expenditures on social welfare programs seemed to hardly make a dent in the problem of the working poor. Rather than getting better, the facts on the ground seemed to indicate quite the reverse. Drawing together what was for the time an impressive array of empirical data to prove his point, Malthus published in 1798 a long pamphlet with the simple title *Essays on Population.* He argued that population will always increase faster than our ability to feed it, with the result being general and lasting misery for the working classes. His two assumptions were paragons of simplicity: "food is necessary to the existence of man [and] the passion between the sexes is necessary and will remain nearly in its present state." In other words, food and sex drive the need for human action. He argued that, since population increases geometrically (2, 4, 8, 16 . . .) whereas food increases only arithmetically (1, 2, 3, 4 . . .), only starvation, war, and forced birth control could keep things in balance. Population would always adjust itself to be at, or just above, the ability of the environment to support it, and no amount of social welfare could change the finite ability of the earth to supply food for an exploding population. Malthus argued that programs aimed at easing the lot of the poor could actually worsen social conditions by enabling poor people to produce yet more children who would then need to be fed by even larger government handouts, a spiral that would eventually bankrupt even the wealthiest nation. He quoted statistics for several European countries that demonstrated their rapid population growth and, in a series of revisions that expanded his long pamphlet into a much longer book, he added still more evidence gathered from his travels across eastern Europe and Russia.

Malthus wasn't content just to identify the problem; he suggested ways to escape the constant struggle of the poor to survive. Understandably for a member of the clergy, he thought that teaching Christian morality to the masses would lead to "moral restraint" and a reduction in the rate of procreation. With the same resources spread among fewer people, more would be able to enter the middle class, where they would develop a taste for comfortable living, a further stimulus to having fewer children. In fact, this is roughly what happened in northern Europe over the second half of the twentieth century: the standard of living increased dramatically and the birth rate dropped. Malthus's error was in failing to appreciate that increased agricultural production could enable the masses to be fed for long enough for social change to occur. Science gave society time to adapt.

The notion that consumption would outstrip resources was the idea behind another famous work published in 1972—nearly two centuries after Malthus—by a think tank known as the Club of Rome. Using the newly developed technique of system dynamics, *The Limits to*

Growth described a set of computer models that looked at the interplay between population growth, resource availability, pollution, and other factors affecting social well-being. The authors found that their model accurately described the state of the world's economy from 1900 to 1970, a period of unprecedented growth and discovery. However, as they ran the model into the future they found that the runaway demands of an unchecked population led to stagnation, starvation, and collapse—remarkably similar to the predictions made by Malthus's far simpler methods. They looked at a range of estimates of how much oil, arable soil, clean water, and other resources we might have available, but every run of the model resulted in the same pattern of rapid population growth followed by abrupt collapse, the only variable being just when that collapse occurred. (Using what they viewed as wildly optimistic numbers, they predicted that such a collapse could occur before the year 2100.) Often cited as purveyors of doom and gloom, the authors took great pains to discuss the limitations of their model and to say that, rather than predict the future, its main purpose was to begin a serious discussion on the need to *plan* our future, and the sooner the better. They fully understood that humankind is creative and adaptive; one need only look at rising agricultural yields and the dissemination of birth control methods to see how we were already responding to the problem. But they argued that these advances were only staving off the inevitable, and that we should use this time to design and achieve an equilibrium between population and resources, an equilibrium that would be sustainable into the indefinite future.

It was the authors' implicit belief in an equilibrium policy, a static solution that would enable us to live happily ever after, that sunk the conclusions of *The Limits to Growth*. Given the nature of our species, it seems clear that we will never be content with the status quo, no matter how comfortable and logical it might seem. No society, regardless of how rich or powerful, has managed to remain in equilibrium for more than a few generations. Rome was far from depleting its resources and was a paragon of logical government, yet it ultimately collapsed, more as a result of internal corruption than any external pressure. The United States had more than enough to keep it busy at the end of the nineteenth century, but we still found a reason to go to war with Spain. The fact is that population pressure and the availability of resources are only two factors, albeit critical ones, that influence social evolution. Other things, including fear, ambition, and revenge, also influence events. Peace must not be confused with paralysis, passive inaction that is contrary to our competitive human nature. Our task is to find ways to satisfy our drive to compete and push the limits of the possible, ways that avoid killing one another in large numbers.

It's more than our inability to sit still; our very nature is constantly changing. Each generation brings new individuals to the table, people with a unique combination of drives and skills, people who want to put their own stamp on history. What would have happened in the twentieth century if there had been no Winston Churchill to inspire resistance to Hitler? What would have happened if there had been no Hitler, if the Weimar Republic had somehow succeeded in converting the wreckage of imperial Germany into a stable democracy? Suppose the last Russian tsar was a standout diplomat and social reformer, and the communists gave up trying to get a foothold in Russia? Would either of the world wars or the subsequent cold war have occurred? Or would other cataclysms have taken their place? One of the hallmarks of any practical plan to reduce the probability of mass violence will be the recognition that the world is, and will likely remain, in a state of flux, constantly adjusting to physical and human changes. It would be incredibly naïve of us to think that we could construct the perfect plan, one so accurate that we could just check off the boxes as we sail into a secure future. Military planners understand this when they say that the purpose of deliberate planning is not to find the perfect way forward but to identify as many contingencies as possible, better enabling them to adapt when things go awry. By thinking of all the things that *might* happen, and thinking about how we might respond, we put ourselves in a better position to anticipate trouble and head it off before it gets out of hand.

The remainder of the book will focus on practical means for the reduction of mass violence using three sets of tools: diplomacy, economics, and military force. We will look at what has worked in the past, and what has failed to work, as a guide to the construction of future plans. It is worth remembering that, while we are indeed talking about the "big picture," there is little practical value in pie-in-the-sky idealism, an appeal for some global consciousness raising that will magically make everyone live together in harmony. We must do more than renounce all violence in the hope that others will follow suit and that war and genocide will simply disappear. As the example earlier in this chapter suggests, to abdicate all violence could well allow ruthless individuals to have their way, stimulating the very thing that we hope to suppress.

Nonviolent resistance works admirably well when the society in which it occurs has a degree of morality sufficient to respect the rights of the resisters; it fails when those in power lack such restraint, when they consider violence to be a viable means toward an end or, worse yet, a virtue. While I respect the convictions of true pacifists, I see no reason whatsoever to believe that, without positive action, we will not see repeated instances of mass slaughter. Yes, there is a line beyond which one becomes immoral, when you cross over to the dark side and become what you hoped to suppress, but seldom does history present us with a clear decision between nonviolence and barbarism. We must seek a path that recognizes the potential for human violence and uses all means to minimize the possibility of that violence getting out of hand. I believe that those people who stand by and watch violence happen, smug in their own refusal to commit a violent act no matter what the provocation, have some of the blood of the victims on their hands. Not to act in such a situation is to allow even worse things to happen.

Planning doesn't require or even assume perfection: an imperfect plan that achieves something is better than no plan at all. And we have a key advantage over our predecessors in that we have vastly more knowledge of ourselves and our social institutions than ever before. Malthus had to collect his own data about population trends in Europe, and *The Limits to Growth* was done at a time when we knew much less about the distribution of resources on Earth than we do now. We can use our knowledge to guide us, to avoid pitfalls and exploit successes. But why should we even try? Why do we think that we have any chance of succeeding when so many others have failed? *Because we do not have a choice.* To continue on our current course is to accept what fate brings us, and fate has been unkind to us over the past century.

the tools of change:
what we can do to prevent
mass violence

politics and diplomacy as tools for peace

Lest maddened by the lust for power,
we shall ourselves destroy . . .
—VERSE FROM A VICTORIAN HYMN

As a theoretical physicist, I have always been interested in mathematical models of complex phenomena. Even after decades spent doing science, it never ceases to amaze me that, using just paper and pencil (or computers), it is possible to calculate what is found in nature. I have modeled things as simple as a single atom and as complex as a nuclear explosion, sometimes with good results and sometimes with the realization that real life is more complicated than my simple equations would predict. However, I have always found that the rigor required of mathematical modeling has helped me to clarify my thinking, forced me to systematically write down each assumption, and to look deeper for what might be missing.

A lifelong interest in philosophy, combined with a career spent around nuclear weapons, has led me to try to apply some of the same rigor to the bigger issues affecting humanity. If we really are at a crossroads, a turning point in the history of our species, how can we best think about our choices? How can we avoid making erroneous assumptions about what is possible or practical, assumptions that might be based more on preconceived notions than solid facts?

Several years ago, I had the idea to combine my interests in modeling and philosophy by using computers to simulate human society, especially the effect of different ethical systems on social performance. I wanted to simulate more than just *what* people do but *why* they do it. Are there fundamental reasons why we act the way that we do and why our social organizations are the way that we find them? Are some ethical systems better than others at reducing violence? No computer model could include all of the complexities of human behavior, but just the rigor of setting up the simulation might help us better understand the problem.

My computer program described a collection of people who ate, slept, mated, and explored their environment according to a fixed set of rules. I put them on an isolated island and arranged them in social groups such as families and villages. What would happen in this artificial society if all of the participants shared altruistically with one another or, conversely, what would happen if everyone was a thief, taking whatever they wanted without regard to the suffering that it caused others? How about if a leader was incredibly charismatic, attracting followers to do his or her bidding? Or, what would happen if that leader was aggressive and greedy, abusing the population for personal gain? I thought of this as a kind of "computational philosophy" or "experimental ethics," an approach perhaps a bit more rigorous than the traditional verbal debate and one that might be more appealing to the type of analytical minds involved in setting national policy. To lend credibility to what might otherwise be amusing computer games, I compared the results of my simulations to a number of real-life societies, often with very encouraging agreement.

A number of books and articles have appeared in recent years describing the benefits of sharing and cooperation. It seems that people in every society share what they have with others, so if there is a set of universal human behaviors, then sharing appears to be among them. My simulations showed the expected result that sharing was an effective way of distributing scarce resources in a group, ensuring that everyone got enough to survive and hence to enable them to mate and produce the next generation. However, I found that stealing was *equally effective* at distributing resources. One could either share things with others or take things from them—either behavior resulted in a roughly even distribution of vital materials. So why do human beings share rather than steal, why is it that no society ever encountered consisted only of thieves? My simulations suggested that the answer lay more in the social aspects of sharing than in its economic function. Most people are grateful when someone gives them something and they are angry when someone steals from them. If human beings were able to live on their own, there might be no difference, but the fact that we need companionship changes the equation in a dramatic way. Sharing is more than an economic transaction. We share to create a web of mutual obligations within society, a web that provides us the comfort of knowing that others care about us and will take care of us if we are in need. There is a reason why people act the way that they do.

One topic that I found particularly fascinating was the effect of tolerance on social development. What happens when, in the interest of social harmony, you forgive occasional transgressions rather than retaliating in an eye-for-an-eye manner? We normally think of tolerance as a virtue, but how much forgiveness is a good thing before the bad guys begin to win? Hundreds of simulations told me that my model society could only survive with either very little tolerance or very high tolerance; in between there was a high probability that the society would collapse. Digging into the details, I found that people in intolerant societies quickly corrected bad behavior among their peers, with the result that everyone shared and treated one another equitably. Conversely, at very high tolerance levels, there were no consequences to stealing and everyone could get away with everything. The result was a population of thieves. The problem at intermediate values of tolerance was that sharers were so abused by thieves that, over time, they died out. That left a population of thieves who, unfortunately, couldn't tolerate *one another* enough to mate and reproduce. The result was population extinction—the collapse of a model civilization.

This theoretical result became much more interesting when I discovered that *all* known egalitarian societies—those without hierarchical governments and the type that I was modeling—practiced strict intolerance and were relentless in the suppression of bad behavior. When two people had a problem with each other, they settled the score themselves, usually without delay. Cultures as different as the Aborigines of Australia, the Inuit, the Polynesians, and the Bushmen of the Kalahari all behaved this way. I wondered if the reason was that alternate systems (namely, higher degrees of tolerance) were simply not viable.

While my simulations were very simple compared to real human behavior, they had enough detail to suggest that some modes of behavior really *are* better than others. Some ethical systems lead to societies that are remarkably stable over many generations, and others lead to privation and collapse. And before you discount these results as only applicable to "primitive societies," think again about the horrible carnage that "civilized" nations have wrought. The country of Beethoven and Bach was also the country of Hitler and Himmler. The Japanese culture that prized quiet contemplation was the same one that ravaged Nanking. The same Americans who fought so persistently to abolish slavery also fought to exterminate the American Indians. We are more alike than we are different, human animals who prefer to live in close proximity to one another and who are prone to using violence to achieve our ends. The question to be addressed in this chapter is what we might do to organize ourselves *as a species* to lessen the likelihood that mass violence will occur, especially violence involving weapons of mass destruction. How can we best avoid the type of population extinction that afflicted some of my artificial societies? And how can the United States, the most powerful nation in the world, help this process and avoid falling into the traps of arrogance and imperialism that corrupted our predecessors on the world stage?

Our world is a society of societies. Individual people are members of families, which are members of clans, which are often clustered in regions, which are part of countries, some of which belong to international bodies. We like the feeling of belonging to something, especially when it is something that we admire, an organization whose principles we adhere to voluntarily because we think that they are right and uplifting. The challenge in human organization is much more than deciding between anarchy and totalitarianism—both are obvious extremes that have caused much misery in the past—but the identification of something in between that is stable and effective over the long term. How can we live together and achieve our full potential while minimizing the possibility of mass violence? What set of organizational principles and rules would optimize our quality of life and minimize the prospect of large-scale violence?

Twenty years ago, any discussion of mass violence would have focused on the nation-state, for only countries had the resources to inflict mass damage on society. Today, we are much more worried about international terrorism, groups that have no national loyalties whatever. Is the era of the nation-state over? Is it about to be replaced by a

chaotic set of groups that span national borders and act without regard to the health and welfare of their geographical neighbors? I think
not. Despite all of our progress toward the creation of a global village,
most people in the world still use nationality as a principal form of
self-identification. Terrorists may consider themselves independent
of any nation, but they still exist *somewhere*, in some country, and they
depend on the resources and people of that country to achieve their
ends. Also, the continued presence of huge arsenals of conventional
and nuclear weapons indicates that we still need to pay attention to
international relations. Finally, nation-states still offer the best means
to address mass violence in a systematic and organized manner since
they have the resources, the reach, and the responsibility to effect
change. In discussing how we might use politics and diplomacy to
create a safer future, we begin with a short digression of how the international environment came to be the way that we find it today.

One of the most fundamental rules affecting modern international
relations arose from the Treaty of Westphalia, signed in 1648 to end
the Thirty Years War, a particularly bloody conflict that killed over
40 percent of the population of some parts of Germany. Essentially a
fight over the rights of the Holy Roman Empire mixed with a strong
dose of religious factionalism, the war was fought with both sides believing that their cause was more important than the political boundaries of Europe. Numerous peace conferences were held over a span
of more than a decade, each failing to satisfy one or more precondi-
tions set by the combatants. Even when the final treaty was established, senior French and Spanish diplomats refused to meet
face-to-face because they could not agree on who would enter the
room first.

The breakthrough idea in the Treaty of Westphalia was the concept of national sovereignty, something that we take for granted today but which was relatively novel at the time. Each nation-state was to be considered sovereign and equal on the international stage; what that nation did within its own borders was its own concern, not to be interfered with by others. It was wrong for one country to attack a sovereign state without some outstanding reason, usually one relating to its own self defense.

And it worked. Order was put into a situation that was approaching international chaos, allowing governments to focus their attention on constructive pursuits rather than worry about the threat of imminent invasion. But serious problems still remained. The Treaty of Westphalia had the effect of reducing violence *between* nations but tolerating it *within* nations. National sovereignty allowed governments to literally get away with murder inside their own borders, with very little that well-meaning neighbors could do to help. It is just this difficulty of crossing levels of organization—from the societies *within* nations to the society *of* nations—that so vexes world leaders today. The government of a city or a nation may take measures to reduce domestic violence, but it can't prevent international warfare, whereas an international body such as the United Nations can try to resolve disputes between countries but is almost powerless to address genocide within a sovereign state. Another problem with the Treaty of Westphalia, sometimes overlooked by modern political scientists, is that it was designed to solve problems within a specific environment—namely, in western Europe—where the concept of "national sovereignty" makes sense. It was and is much less applicable in parts of the world where people identify themselves with tribes and where the concept of nation-state seems as odd as absolute monarchy seems to modern Americans.

Until the twentieth century, there was no standing organization that could resolve the differences of governments about borders, natural resources, colonies, and other matters that frequently led to war. People in indigenous egalitarian societies took justice into their own hands; nations did the same to resolve their disagreements. (The Treaty of Westphalia required a nation to have a strong justification to attack its neighbor, but creative minds seldom had to labor long to devise an excuse.) It took the shock of World War I to make people realize that the society of nations needed some form of leadership; the horror of the trenches in this "war to end all wars" was so great that most governments accepted the need to cede some of their national sovereignty in the hope that a future war could be averted. President Woodrow Wilson proposed the League of Nations as a forum for international affairs, one in which potential combatants could come to make their cases before their peers and hopefully resolve their differences without resort to bloodshed. Alas, it was Wilson's own country that rejected the idea of an international organization with binding authority, the argument in Congress being that there was no need for a country as powerful as the United States to put itself under the yoke of any foreign body, especially one dominated by Europeans who seemed constantly at war with one another. With two oceans to insulate us and our enormous industrial capacity, we didn't need anyone to tell us how to run our affairs.

World War II sufficiently elevated the level of violence in warfare, especially violence involving civilian populations, to cause the dominant powers to again attempt an international society, this time one with binding rules of behavior. The creators of the United Nations tried to fix some of the problems that doomed the League of Nations, especially the notion that every country had an equal vote in the decision process. The five senior victorious nations in the war were given permanent membership on a Security Council, with the authority to veto any measure that they found inimical to their own interests, something that happened with great frequency during the cold war. Smaller nations were given a say in the General Assembly, through their participation in myriad panels and international organizations, and by rotating membership on the Security Council. It was a compromise, one that attempted to create a venue where nations were (in principle) *required* to seek approval before attacking anyone, where the internal affairs of a country could be exposed to world view, and where the plight of the disenfranchised poor could have a hearing.

Unfortunately, the unwieldy decision-making mechanisms of the United Nations almost guaranteed a would-be offender a period of days, weeks, months, or even years to dance around threatened sanctions. This happened in the Sudan in 2004 when European countries delayed action partly under pressure of corporate interests tied to the Sudanese government. For these reasons and others, one might conclude that the United Nations is ineffective at preventing mass violence, and that it actually *subverts* the ability of responsible nations to step in and fix obvious problems. How absurd, goes this line of reasoning, to have the leadership of committees simply rotate among nations so that Libya, a country that *admitted* to supporting terrorism, might find itself chairing the Committee on Human Rights. And, echoing the argument against the League of Nations, why should the United States submit itself to regulation or censure by the thuggish regimes of Côte d'Ivoire or North Korea? Why should we have to wait for a country to attack us before we take measures to defend ourselves? From one perspective, there *isn't* any reason for the United States to cede authority to anyone else; we are so powerful, compared to any and all other nations, that we can do as we please. However, the exercise of a completely unilateral foreign policy would be incredibly costly. It pays to cooperate. The only question is how best to do so.

Without some form of leadership, including the ability to enforce decisions, it is difficult to see how the United Nations can achieve its full potential. However, such leadership might come perilously close to a form of world government that I believe is well outside the comfort zone of most of the world's population. Most people feel the need to belong to a social group; at present, that need is met at the highest level by the nation-state. I strongly suspect, but cannot prove, that the majority are unwilling to have their country give up its sovereign rights to a world government, fearing that their interests could be lost in the drive toward the least common denominator. As an example, just look at the years of effort that have been devoted to achieving the European Union, an organization still working through constitutional issues, questions of defense cooperation, and other items basic to any government body. From an economic standpoint, a united Europe makes good sense, yet attachments to farm subsidies, local working habits, and other regional issues constantly threaten to unravel the hardest fought agreements. Southeast Asia has yet to achieve any real degree of integration even though each country has much to gain by pooling its resources. For all of our progress toward a global community, we still find our comfort zone closest to home.

In contrast to the United Nations, the United States sees itself as a country of *action*, one that *wants* to see change and one that is willing to take risks to achieve that change. As a case in point, after the terrorist attacks of 2001, our natural impulse to *do something* went into overdrive—the time for talking was over, we said. President Bush summed up the feelings of many Americans when he said that other countries were either with us or against us (an ironic echo of Lenin's exhortation in the latter stages of the Russian Revolution) and that we would brook no interference in uprooting the terrorists wherever they might be. There was enormous pressure on the president to take action, to strike back after the cowardly attacks. At a Washington dinner party I attended in October of that year, people wondered how long the president could *delay* attacking Afghanistan before Congress and the people stepped in and demanded it. And, before you prescribe a dose of political Valium for the United States, remember that this same energy and restlessness created the world's foremost economy, its most advanced technology, and a vibrant culture that is emulated from Berlin to Beijing.

The events of September 11, 2001, did more than prompt an angry reaction from the American people—they galvanized the creation of a new vision for the post–cold war period, along with a policy for its implementation. For more than a decade we wandered through a landscape of uncertainty, dubbing it the "new world order" for lack of a better name. As Americans, we were elated at our victory over communism (which might, with more accuracy, be described as the self-initiated collapse of an unworkable system), but we were uncertain as to what we should do with our new position. I saw this myself when, in preparing to write this book, I asked dozens of senior leaders in Washington about their vision for the future. Given our tremendous freedom of action, where do we want the world to go and what are we willing to do to help get it there? Again and again I found that people just didn't know what to say, answering my question with vague notions of a "brighter future" or stale repeats of dated ideology.

It was President George W. Bush who offered the first comprehensive vision for the post–cold war world, a vision that addressed the most pressing issues of our time and especially the need to reduce the threat of mass violence. As is the case with most profound ideas, the president's proposal was eminently simple and understandable: the world would be a better place if more countries had democratic governments. Democratic governments don't go to war with other democratic governments, and if the leader becomes too dictatorial inside the country, then he or she can be replaced in the next election. The United States is an example of the power of popular opinion—a success story that others might emulate as peers and partners in working toward a better world.

President Bush's belief in the power of democracy was based on a widely accepted bloc of political theory, namely, that the main cause of international violence is failures in the *internal* governance of nations rather than the lack of *world* governance. Dictators, so the argument goes, are greedy and prone to attack their neighbors, while democracies are slower to go to war since the leader typically has to first secure the approval of the legislature and, ultimately, must explain his or her actions to the people. The notion that the government is ultimately responsible to the people imparts a transparency to financial affairs and indeed to all the actions of the government, a transparency that is a strong deterrent to malfeasance. Democratic governments are likely to invest their resources more wisely than autocracies, avoiding the pillaging of national economies that can lead to violent internal discord. Should the people lose confidence that their interests are being served, there is always the option of trying a different path in the next election.

Democracy goes a long way toward solving the conundrum created by the Treaty of Westphalia: that national sovereignty reduces the probability of interstate violence but does little to regulate internal abuses. Democracy reduces the probability of violence between nation-states *and* the probability of violence within a country. It avoids the thorny problem of world governance and it maintains the comfort zone of people who are proud of their national customs and who wish to identify with their country as their paramount social group. Democracy is a workable balance, enabling people to reach their full potential while providing vital checks against abuses. If the government of every country were democratic, then many of the problems that we grapple with today—war and genocide principal among them—would be much less frequent and the United Nations could serve as a useful meeting place rather than a consensus-driven decision body.

In his first inauguration speech, President Bush emphasized the need for humility, engagement in the international community as a partner, and an understanding and sometimes acceptance of political differences. His defense policy focused on transforming the military away from the massive formations designed to fight the cold war toward a responsive force more suited to police actions and humanitarian missions. Much of his energy was devoted to domestic issues, including tax reform, energy policy, and education.

All of this changed abruptly with the terrorist attacks of September 11, 2001, which were as traumatic for the president as for all other Americans. An honorable man, Bush saw the attacks as cowardly. As someone who believed in the inherent goodness of the United States, he was shocked that anyone would attack innocent civilians and then gloat over the carnage. And most important, he saw Al Qaeda as an evil force bent on depriving people of the rights that so many had fought and died for in the twentieth century. There could be no common ground with such people.

Even more worrying to the president was the possibility that Osama bin Laden was pursuing weapons of mass destruction. Intelligence reports indicated that Al Qaeda was interested in chemical, biological, and even nuclear weapons. They had plenty of money, were adept users of the Internet, and had sympathetic technical advisers around the world. Bush's immediate response to this threat was to eliminate terrorist bases of operations in Afghanistan and begin a persistent manhunt for their senior leaders. However, he knew that this was only a first step, and that a longer-term strategy needed to be developed to address the fundamental causes of global terrorism. He began to look for an overarching principle that could guide the country, one in which our natural proclivity for action and for fixing problems could be exercised, an approach that would lay a solid foundation for a more peaceful future. With a deep personal belief in the benefits of democracy, Bush began to construct a new policy for the United States, a proactive policy of encouraging the spread of freedom and self-determination around the world. He reasoned that when people had the right to choose their leaders and, indirectly, the policies of their governments, they would be less likely to tolerate terrorists and the regimes that harbor them. Also, with democracy would come the ability for people to better themselves through their own peaceful labors, making them much less susceptible to the lures of violent organizations. While domestic and international critics chastised the Bush administration for its arrogance and unilateralist approach, it did what very few (if any) world leaders have done: it presented a rational plan to escape the seemingly inescapable curse of both intranational and international violence.

Bush's next move was much less obvious. The occupation of Iraq was a huge gamble, and the dice will continue to roll for some time. While the principal reason given for our ouster of Saddam Hussein was the worry that he had, or was seeking to acquire, weapons of mass destruction, there was another, more far-reaching rationale. President Bush saw the removal of the Baath regime as an opportunity to create an island of democracy in the volatile but vital Middle East, an opportunity to convert the region's worst trouble spot into the most hopeful area for the future. He wanted to create a democratic nation that could serve as an example to its neighbors and a potential friend to the United States in a dangerous neighborhood.

Many people are convinced that we acted hastily in Iraq, before international pressure and inspections had a chance to play out. They believe that our objectives could have been met without the huge cost in lives and money that the war has entailed. International sanctions were never 100 percent effective due to extensive smuggling, but over time it is possible that Saddam's regime would have collapsed under its own weight. However, even if that happened, it would have been necessary to ensure the exit of his sons, who by all accounts were even more vicious than he was, and the other Baath loyalists who were waiting in the wings to enjoy the fruits of absolute power. The patient approach required faith that some more moderate government would spontaneously arise to assume power, in that country that had so long suffered under dictatorship. Alternately, we might have played a waiting game until Saddam convinced himself that he had to make some grand move to demonstrate his continued power, a move that would have united the world behind action in the same way that his invasion of Kuwait did. We will never know what might have happened.

Several commentators have contrasted our experience in postwar Iraq with the very different situation that prevailed in Japan and Germany after World War II. Such comparisons are misleading, however, since the situations were very different in a number of ways. First, both Germany and Japan were coherent cultural units with populations that clearly identified themselves as Japanese and German. Iraq was an artificial country, a collection of tribes brought together in a shotgun wedding by Great Britain and France. Second, Germany and Japan had cultures that emphasized social discipline, priding themselves on an orderly society with a strong respect for authority. Iraq's history was so turbulent, and its governments so irresponsible, that its people had little faith or trust in the central administration. Third, Germany and Japan both realized that they had been *defeated*. It is questionable that, even with tens of thousands of foreign soldiers on its soil, Iraq considers itself a defeated nation. Finally, the critics do have a point when they observe that planning for postwar Germany and Japan began much sooner, and involved a great deal more talent, than did postwar planning in Iraq. In hindsight, the Defense Department's exclusion of professionals from the State Department, people who knew the Middle East and the challenges of nation building, was ill advised to say the least. The facts painfully demonstrate that the Pentagon's close control of everything to do with Iraq failed to win the peace. Postwar Iraq presented and continues to present a different set of challenges than postwar Germany and Japan, but all three illustrate the wisdom of Jean-Jacques Rousseau's sage comment, "To conquer is easier than to administer."

Even in less challenging environments than Iraq, there are serious stumbling blocks to be faced in implementing President Bush's vision. First, many attempts at democracy have ended with a strong man either seizing power or, in some cases, being asked to take absolute power to restore order. Second, there is a lot of work to be done to bring the world's population to the point where people know enough to make informed choices. Third, there are parts of the world where the attraction of hierarchical governance is deeply ingrained in the psyche of the people.

With regard to democracy being replaced by absolute government, there is abundant historical data to toss cold water on the most devout democrat. Fledgling democracies in Greece, Rome, France,

Germany, Russia, and many other countries failed to hold their own against the lure of strong and supposedly efficient central leadership. And it wasn't always a case of a nefarious dictator seizing power from a freedom-loving people; in many cases the problem was that democracy, for all its attraction, just wasn't getting the job done. In some cases, the transition back to strong central authority was so gradual as to be hardly noticed, the government accumulating more and more power until it was almost indistinguishable from a dictatorship. As Winston Churchill observed in his wonderful (if somewhat biased) *History of the English-Speaking Peoples*, Great Britain and the United States seem to have been the first countries to have hit on a winning formula for government that balanced operational efficiency with accountability to the people. While hardly innocent of imperial expansion, and while they did great damage to indigenous populations around the world, Great Britain and the United States largely avoided the self-initiated wars of conquest that typified absolute governments. Perhaps it was only that we replaced military aggression with commercial expansion, but the effect was still a reduction in the number of instances of state-sponsored violence. So far, democracy seems to be the best thing going for stopping mass destruction.

The secret to the success of Great Britain and the United States may lie in the second challenge to implementing democracy—the need for an educated population. In a simple egalitarian society, it might be more important to know how to interact with your neighbors than to be able to analyze complex policy decisions. But when a country has the power to reach beyond its own borders, its people had better understand at least a little bit about the probable outcome of their actions. A population that might be comfortable to live at home under a king or "president for life" might be less comfortable if that ruler took the country into a ruinous war, did something to encourage invasion by another country, or provoked devastating economic sanctions by the United Nations. Democracy can only work if the people have enough information, and the proper rational skills, to make a decision. However, education alone does not assure the success of democracy, as was painfully illustrated in twentieth century wars between industrial nations.

An even greater challenge for global democracy is our third reason for concern, the fact that strong government has a deep hold on the psyche of many people around the world. People who live under repressive regimes are just as clever and perceptive as everyone else—they understand that it would be better to live in a democracy. However, many people living under authoritarian governments understand how to live in those systems and fear the chaos that could accompany their collapse. I saw such fear demonstrated when, after a convivial dinner at a Russian friend's house in 1994, the topic turned to the future of that country. The Russians are great philosophizers who love to talk about the sweeping issues of life and, since they were going through a profound transformation, the topic was only natural for an evening's discussion. The thinking among the Americans was that Russia's enormous human and material resources would allow it to bounce back relatively quickly, perhaps in a decade, but most of the Russians thought that real progress would take a generation or more. We debated various issues over glasses of homemade cherry wine until our elderly hostess burst out with, "Ah, if we only had Stalin again—Stalin would make things right!" I was stunned. Here was an intelligent woman, someone who had lived through the worst of the purges, wishing for the return of a man who killed more Russians than Hitler. Stalin was an evil man who eliminated anyone who was even a *potential* threat to his absolute power. My hostess remembered the faces of the slave laborers who built her city, the dread of a knock on the door in the middle of the night, the constant worry of being reported for "anti-Soviet activities" by a neighbor or even a family member. The reason that she idolized Stalin was a fear deep within the Russian cultural consciousness, a fear of returning to a time of troubles when the country was without order and governance. Almost anything—including a brutal dictatorship—would be preferable to that.

It is manifestly clear that people want a say in how they are governed. About half the world's countries are already ruled by nominally democratic governments. The real debate is how to promote democracy fast enough to avoid ever-increasing violence as ever more powerful weapons come into the hands of irresponsible governments, groups, and individuals. How do we organize the society of nations in a way that mass violence, either between nations or within a single nation state, is less likely to happen? By all accounts, it's going to take a while to reach that ideal situation where the combination of internal democracy and respect for the sovereign rights of states prevents war and genocide. So there is a problem about what to do in the meantime.

But wait a moment. Why is there any need for the United States to spend its treasure on promoting democracy when the problem is already being taken care of through the globalization of the world economy and the spread of a common culture through the Internet? How could the ultranationalism that precipitated World Wars I and II happen in a world where millions of British, French, and Germans read the same news from the same websites, where they drive one another's cars, eat one another's cuisine, and watch one another's television programs? After all, even the military-industrial complex has become multinational, with subsidiaries around the world.

While this may seem like a good argument, it has several flaws. First, globalization is primarily an economic activity without much in the way of strategic direction. Companies send work offshore to cut their costs and increase their profits—geopolitical strategy is seldom a factor in their decision process. While there have been some encouraging signs that multinational corporations are paying attention to the working conditions of their foreign employees, even that trend has had more to do with protests from American consumers than from the altruistic values of the corporation. Our priorities are mixed: blue-collar workers object to their manufacturing jobs being shipped overseas, but they love the low prices at discount superstores that buy almost exclusively from those same foreign manufacturers.

President Clinton, a tireless proponent of the inevitability of globalization, is certainly right that it is an idea whose time has come. It would be foolish to think that, with the now oft-mentioned improvements in communication and transportation, we could cut the myriad ties that join people and organizations around the world. Nor would we want to, since there is evidence that increased engagement in the global enterprise has raised the standard of living of most of the third world. Even in the poorest countries, life expectancy is increasing and infant mortality is decreasing. However, as with most tools, the ultimate result of globalization will depend on how and for what we use it, whether we consider it only as a means for profit generation or as a means of transforming despotic states into peaceful democracies.

While globalization has already brought people closer together, any enthusiasm over its ability to avert mass violence should be tempered by a recollection of its previous failures, the most spectacular of which was World War I. In 1910, the British social thinker Norman Angell argued that war between the European powers was impossible and any conflict that did break out would be short-lived. His reasoning was that the major powers had such tightly interlocking economies that none could sustain isolation for any length of time. Germany needed raw materials, England needed markets, and Russia needed to import technology. Such was the interdependence of these nations that a devastating war between them was effectively impossible. In numerous editions of his highly popular book *The Great Illusion*, Angell presented ever more charts and tables to make his case, but the events of August 1914 proved him disastrously wrong. To cite only one reason, Germany didn't *want* to depend upon other countries for its supply of raw materials, a dependency that it considered a strategic weakness. Yes, countries had tightly interconnected economies, but the nature of European governments at the time made them risk all on the outcome of a war.

However, things are different today from the way that they were in 1914, in at least three ways. First, the degree of interconnectedness is vastly greater than it was then. Today, "global" means more than one country needing the natural resources and markets of other countries. Multinational companies are so spread out that it's hard to assign a nationality to them. Second, most people have a much better understanding of the world and better access to information than was the case a century ago. Third, the United Nations at least offers a venue for airing grievances, a venue that was sadly lacking when kings and emperors took the world over the brink. However, while some things are different, others are very much the same. Just as imperial governments manipulated the opinions of their people to support going to war, terrorists capture the hearts and minds of millions of people in the disenfranchised Islamic world, emphasizing grievances and promising a better life through violent action. Even when people had access to accurate sources of information, many people chose to listen to the terrorists' account of September 11 rather than the BBC, CNN, or other factual news organizations. Globalization is certainly a trend in the right direction, but to rely on it to reduce the occurrences of mass violence is little more than hoping that "things will somehow turn out all right."

Presidents Bush and Clinton each had a vision of the future. The fundamental difference between the two was that President Bush believed that positive action, including the selective use of force, could accelerate the achievement of peace through democracy. President Clinton believed that globalization would eventually achieve the same goal, albeit more slowly. One can debate whether the short-term violence implicit in President Bush's approach would result in more or fewer total deaths than President Clinton's more patient process of globalization, one in which wars and genocide could occur unchecked along the way to an integrated and interconnected world. The jury is still out and likely to remain so for some time. However, President Bush's approach has the advantage of appealing to a natural American instinct to *do something*, to step up to the plate and try to make things better. We have never been a passive people, willing to stand by and hope for the best. We believe in ourselves and our mission and we are willing to accept the occasional stumble along the road to a better future. Many Americans disagree with the path that was taken by the Bush administration, especially the use of preemptive force in Iraq, but few people believe that we could or should retreat into isolationism, hoping somehow that the world will leave us alone. Superpowers can't hide.

What is common about the approaches of Presidents Bush and Clinton is that each relies on some form of engagement to construct a better future. We cannot ignore the world, satisfied that our military superiority can defend us against any aggressor. The world is too complex, too subtle, and the forces of destruction that can be arrayed against us are too powerful to allow us to retreat behind the vast Atlantic and Pacific. Failure to engage will only make us a target, allowing a potential adversary time to prepare his attack. We can no longer afford to delay a response until the problem has become acute and much more difficult to solve. Nor can we afford the costs of repeated military preemption at every hint of a threat. There is a happy medium and our job is to find it.

Engagement as the preeminent member of the global community does not mean that we should ignore our own interests or that we must soften our conviction in the benefits of democracy. Rather, it *enhances* our ability to get our message across to anyone who is willing to listen. The best way to get other nations to listen to us is to get into the same room and listen to *them*. Again, this doesn't mean that we can't fight back if we think that the other side is wrong. Daniel Patrick Moynihan, an ambassador to the United Nations, was nonetheless a fierce critic of that body, not because he didn't believe in the value of international engagement, but because he refused to stand by while petty tyrants criticized the United States to divert attention from their own crimes. Engagement is an indicator of our strength rather than of our weakness. No other country has the freedom of action enjoyed by the United States, a freedom of action enabled by our confidence in our convictions and our unparalleled military and economic position in the world.

Can we force our will on other people? Yes, if we're strong enough, but in doing so we create an environment in which we are constantly on the lookout for bad behavior, constantly spending our energy on keeping everyone in line rather than advancing toward our objective. Forcing our will on other cultures can build up resentment that could explode with disastrous consequences, making the situation worse. A real leader recognizes that his or her biggest challenge is to convince people that they *want* to behave in a certain way, to enlist them as willing and enthusiastic participants in getting the job done. Everyone knows that it is much better to motivate people to perform than to have them work grudgingly out of fear of punishment. What is true in a society of individual people is also true in a society of nations. While we are the richest and most powerful country in the world, we comprise less than 5 percent of the world's population. The United States lacks the resources and the credibility to go it alone—not even we can afford to repeat the cost of Iraq. Other countries watch carefully what we do, and if our response to every perceived threat is the use of force, we can only assume that they will act accordingly. They will give serious consideration to acquiring weapons of mass destruction, this being the only counter they would have to our military superiority. And we need the help of our friends in dealing with countries we have bad relations with. Sometimes an intermediary can get our message across better than we can.

Engagement in the world community has other advantages. I know of no effective leader who thinks that he or she has the right answer to every problem. The best leaders are good listeners, people who understand their authority as well as their limitations and who look to others for good ideas. Proactive engagement in the international community will help us better understand the needs and concerns of other countries so that we may best apply our time and treasure to solving problems and, in an ideal situation, be more effective at getting other countries to contribute to the cause.

Stronger participation in the international community requires confidence in our objectives and courage to overcome the occasional disappointment. Above all, engagement requires a patience that is difficult in a political environment dominated by short election cycles. We are in the international arena for more than two or four or six years—we are in it for the long haul and we need to act accordingly, much as the Chinese have done with their famous fifty-year outlook.

Finally, engagement helps promote the notion that the United States not only talks the talk but also walks the walk. Other countries resent the United States preaching one thing and then doing another, and this resentment can manifest itself in subtle but persistent ways, making our goals all the more difficult to achieve. Think about this in your own life. Whom do you truly respect and admire—the bully or the saint, the one who tells you what to do or the one who inspires you by example? Which one would you be most willing to help if he or she was in a bind? What companies do you admire—the ones that use sweatshop labor in third-world countries in order to boost their bottom line or the ones that build child care centers for their employees? What countries do you respect—the ones that invade their neighbors to enrich themselves or the ones that are first on the scene with humanitarian relief following a disaster? Now put yourself on the receiving end of these actions. If you're a single parent your loyalty to your company would go up if it provided low-cost after-school care for your children. And if you were one of the tsunami victims of 2004, you would long remember who came to help with food and medical care. Every American sailor knows the legendary hospitality of Australian ports, full of people who remember that the United States was there for them during World War II, now more than two generations in the past.

Contrast these feelings of goodwill with the ceremonies that commemorate the D-day landings. It was only in 2004, more than *two generations* after the end of the war, that a German chancellor was invited to participate, and even then it was deemed inappropriate for him to visit a German cemetery. Think about the damage that was done to the United States' image by the horrific pictures of prisoner abuse in Iraq or the debate about whether we should be bound by the

Geneva Convention. "We were under attack," you might reply, "and we had to defend ourselves. The ends justified the means." But did they really? Is the United States made more secure by having 1.2 billion Muslims distrust our motives? Do you think that young Iraqi men, especially those without jobs or hope, are more likely to resist the temptation to join the insurgency after they have seen photographs of Iraqi soldiers being humiliated and tortured?

We may win the battle in Iraq, which is hardly surprising given our overwhelming military superiority, but assuredly we will lose the war if we abandon those principles that made us the beacon of hope to the world, a country that attracts five times the number of immigrants as the nearest competitor (Germany), a country that hopes to shape the world into a better place. And, let's stop using the justification that Saddam Hussein used even more brutal methods to achieve his ends, a statement that I find totally devoid of moral content. Is our new standard of moral behavior to be a tyrant who killed his own brother and gassed his own people, our idea of morality being that we need only be marginally better than he was? It's much harder for other countries to criticize us when we take the high road, subjecting ourselves to the same norms and requirements we subject others to. There is an occasional cost, to be sure, but the benefits are enormous when integrated over the long term.

Rather than abdicating our power, I advocate an approach that will use that power to best advantage. The United States has the opportunity to truly *lead* the international community, but we can only do that if we are a *part* of that community. President Theodore Roosevelt's advice to "walk softly and carry a big stick" applies to this century as much as it did to the last—our conventional military superiority, backed by our nuclear arsenal, makes it suicidal for any country or group of countries to attack us. From this secure position we can undertake a program of engagement and encouragement of democracy that only we can lead.

What about the frightening prospect that weapons of mass destruction will spread from nation-states to terrorist groups or even individuals? How does proactive engagement aimed at spreading democracy reduce the threat from subnational groups?

In fact, it may be the best way to suppress subnational violence. Most terrorist groups adopt their destructive methods because they see no other means for achieving their objective. More than a religion or political cause, what attracts people to terrorist movements is the opportunity to believe in something, the feeling that they are doing something more important than hanging around on street corners. Without a voice in how policies are developed and implemented in their part of the world, and with a strong suspicion that the United States is actually making their situation more difficult by supporting oppressive regimes, a frustration rises that eventually finds its outlet in religious extremism and violence. Democracy attacks the root causes of terrorism by providing an alternate and *better* means to address problems, providing a degree of hope for the future. Of course there will always be disaffected individuals who use violence as a means to express their frustration, but the hope that comes from democracy will make their job of recruiting followers much more difficult. After all, people who believe that they can make their children's lives better by their own efforts are far less likely to follow zealots whose message is nonproductive hate and whose method is suicide. Is democracy a guarantee against future terrorism? Of course not—no governmental system or technology can be an absolute guarantee against anything. But to forego the good in pursuit of the perfect would be naïve and irresponsible.

———

Many people think of politics as a secret activity conducted in smoke-filled rooms and diplomacy as something that occurs in gilded salons filled with beribboned ambassadors. What can an ordinary person do to influence the course of world affairs? Doesn't it require money, influence, connections, and just plain raw power? In fact, in a democracy an ordinary person can do plenty. The U.S. House of Representatives is filled with well-meaning people who have to be reelected every two years. They are constantly keeping their ear to the ground to see what their constituents think, always worrying that an opponent could seize on a popular issue and unseat them at the ballot box. In many cases, the threshold for taking an issue seriously can be as few as ten letters or phone calls from voters. They figure that if ten people are concerned enough to contact them, there must be hundreds more with similar views. Suppose that ten people from each Congressional district wrote a letter to their representatives— something from the heart. It would not take long for Congress to begin to sense that this topic needs attention. Suppose that thousands of Americans wrote about the civil war in the Congo or the genocide in Sudan. How many lives might have been saved? This isn't just the old activism on a larger scale—"getting involved" in the political process. It is a recognition that unrest in another part of the world might rapidly spread to our own neighborhoods. September 11, 2001, was a wake-up call. As citizens of a democracy, it is time for us to apply the same level of proactive planning to preventing mass violence as we do to other urgent priorities.

economic measures to reduce the probability of mass violence

> This world in arms is not spending money
> alone. It is spending the sweat of its
> laborers, the genius of its scientists, the
> hopes of its children.
> —DWIGHT D. EISENHOWER

When I was doing my graduate studies in physics, I was the very model of a starving student. In addition to taking courses and doing research for my dissertation, I worked as a teaching assistant, a job that was neither especially demanding nor well paid. Even though my income was below the poverty line, I was precluded from accepting any form of public assistance since, by definition, the state paid all its employees a perfectly adequate wage. As a result, there were times when, after paying the rent and buying books, I simply had no money left for food. I remember gathering up small change from around our apartment to buy a pound of ground beef that would last my wife and me the two days until payday; it was a bit embarrassing to stand in line at the supermarket counting out pennies, nickels, and dimes, but it was either that or hunger. I came to endure lunchtimes with a grim resignation—two peanut butter and jelly sandwiches on the least expensive bread along with a few cookies. (Decades passed before I could think again of eating peanut butter and jelly.) When I was asked, during my first job interview at the National Bureau of Standards, if I would like to do work in atomic theory I could hardly contain my enthusiasm at the thought of being paid to do theoretical physics.

Even though we were hard-pressed for a few years, what distinguished my wife and me from other poor people is that we knew that our situation was temporary. After getting a Ph.D., I could look forward to an interesting and comfortable life. Most poor people have little opportunity to raise themselves from the grinding poverty that has always dominated their lives. The free time to enjoy life, the resources to give their children a quality education, and the anticipation of a comfortable retirement all seem forever beyond their reach. They live in dilapidated housing, risk their lives going out at night, and worry about their children being attracted to gangs, drugs, and crime. Perhaps more than any other single factor, it is the absence of hope in their future that draws otherwise peaceful people to violence.

Economists have done a number of studies on the relationship between economic well-being and mass violence, some with quite startling results. You might expect poorer people to be more likely to join in violent political or religious movements than well-to-do people, and societies with greater ethnic diversity to be more prone to violence than those that are ethnically homogeneous. You might also reasonably assume that violence is more prevalent in societies with large disparities in wealth than in more uniform societies. In all of these cases, you would be wrong. Paul Collier of the World Bank did a detailed study of forty-seven civil wars, the most common form of mass conflict in the later part of the twentieth century, and found almost no correlation between the degree of poverty and the probability of war. He found that ethnically diverse countries were *less* likely to experience civil war than those with uniform populations, the reason being that with many small groups there is less likelihood that any one of them will be able to occupy an oppressor position in society.

Societies that have large gaps between rich and poor may be ones with large amounts of popular frustration, but the data suggest that this frustration seldom turns violent. In Saudi Arabia, there is a huge disparity between the incomes of the ruling elite and the general population, yet there seems little likelihood of a mass uprising to correct this inequity. African dictators have pillaged national treasuries for decades without many mass protests. When an uprising does occur, it is likely that the would-be leader is more interested in getting his own share of the plunder than in improving the lot of the common folk.

Terrorist groups draw from all socioeconomic classes, but hardly in an equal manner. Studies have found that the leaders of terrorist organizations often come from middle- or upper-income families. Many have advanced educations and use their skills to convince others of righteous grievances that can, they promise, only be addressed by violence. However, rank-and-file terrorists, the ones who would strap on explosives and blow themselves up in a crowded place, are more often poorly educated and from lower socioeconomic strata than their leaders. A common factor in all levels of terrorist organizations is a frustration with the status quo, a feeling that no means short of violence can achieve needed reform. And this frustration often has an economic aspect, sometimes based on a feeling of hopelessness and sometimes on a desire to correct social injustices.

While it is true that many trouble spots seem to be in poor countries—places like Somalia, Sri Lanka, and the Congo—violence occurs across the economic spectrum. Germany was one of the wealthiest countries before World War I and the Japanese economy was growing at an astonishing pace prior to World War II. Yet in both these cases violence reached unparalleled levels. Germany and Japan had the resources to survive and to provide their citizens with comfortable lives, but in each case they wanted more and were willing to use violence as a means of getting it.

It is important to distinguish between those factors that lead to violence and those that sustain violence once it has started. Violence at every level—from individual homicides to international wars—almost invariably starts with some type of righteous grievance. Most murderers are angry with their victim for some perceived slight. Large-scale violence—from terrorism to civil wars to international conflict—is almost always justified by a righteous grievance. Leaders go to great lengths to convince their followers that the only redress for the injustice is to attack those who perpetrate it. Common grievances include residuals from colonial oppression, inequality between social classes or countries, religious intolerance, threat of attack or genocide, and so forth. In the case of civil wars, the lure of wealth often lies somewhere in the background. It is easy to see through the rhetoric of some succession groups when you notice that the land they want just happens to be the richest part of the country.

While a righteous grievance is often a significant factor in starting a war, hard cash is a necessity in prolonging it. It costs a lot of money to buy the thousands of guns necessary to mount a credible insurgency, to buy food for the troops and distribute the propaganda that provides the justification for fighting. Often this money comes from plundering the natural resources of the country itself, as is the case of diamonds in Africa or timber in Indonesia. The rebels either take over the mines and logging operations themselves or hijack shipments on their way to market. Indeed, there is a strong correlation between the probability of civil war and the availability of natural resources within the country. In Angola the National Union for Total Independence of Angola (UNITA) amassed billions of dollars in reserves, more than enough to fund their war for years. Natural resources can be as much a curse as a blessing to developing countries.

Another important source of funding for violence is contributions from sources well outside the danger zone. Both sides of the sectarian violence in Northern Ireland received significant support from Americans who identified themselves with Catholic and Protestant causes; the same can be said of many other conflicts. It is much easier to exert righteous indignation in Boston and Chicago than to have to live with the situation in Belfast or Croatia. Being far from the conflict allows one to focus on the grievance and to be oblivious to the harm that continued conflict is causing to the people who are living in a combat zone.

While poverty may not be a direct cause of mass violence, more large-scale conflicts seem to occur in poorer countries—at least in recent times. One can point to two reasons for this, one having to do with the strength of governments of wealthy countries and another, perhaps more important, having to do with the satisfaction of their populations. Rich countries can afford effective, well-trained police forces that can keep any uprising inside the legal box. In poor countries, the police are often the enforcement arm of repressive governments and are focused more on extracting money from the population than in protecting their rights. Similarly, the armed forces of rich countries are less likely to rebel or become involved in political disputes than those in poor countries, where soldiers go unpaid for months on end.

But perhaps the most important economic factor associated with large-scale violence lies with the perception of the people. If you think that you lead a comfortable life, if you look forward to advancing as a result of your own labors, and if you are confident that the property that you amass will be protected from unlawful seizure by the government or criminal elements, then you are much more likely to have a vested interest in the status quo, including a rejection of destructive violence that would end your relatively happy existence. True, there will always be the disgruntled individual, the loner who will lash out at the system that he or she thinks is oppressive and unfair, but that individual will have a much more difficult time recruiting supporters in a society where people are generally content than one in which people are frustrated and are willing to use any means, including violence, to create change. Countries that have very high unemployment rates, where young people stand on street corners with little hope for self-improvement, where there is no outlet for the natural human ambition to build and improve, seem to have the highest incidence of violence. One need look no further than the Israeli-Palestinian conflict to see how hopelessness plays into the hands of the organizers of terror and insurrection.

Many of us live our lives in a web of financial arrangements that, if we thought about it, we would find alarmingly complex. We buy our homes by agreeing to pay a bank or mortgage company monthly installments that include an interest payment to make the deal worthwhile to them. We regularly buy items on credit and the retailer fully expects that he or she will receive payment from the credit card company, which in turn expects to be paid by us. The company that we work for may borrow millions of dollars to finance a new production plant, hoping that the profits from that plant will enable it to pay off the original loan and return handsome dividends to shareholders. In short, most people in developed countries live within an economic framework that enables them considerable flexibility in how they live their lives and improve their fortunes.

Contrast this with the situation in many underdeveloped countries where the rule of law is secondary to the power of government officials or the vested interests of the wealthy. As Hernando de Soto demonstrates in his book *The Mystery of Capital*, the lack of a legal framework to define and defend property makes it almost impossible for otherwise enterprising people to fully enjoy the fruits of their labors. People in countries like Peru and the Philippines are enterprising and hard-working, remarkably adept at identifying and exploiting opportunities. But they are hobbled in their development by the lack of a system that enables them to accumulate wealth and to use that wealth to practical advantage. Take the case of building a shop in a small village. In some countries, the official bureaucracy is so complex that it can take years—even decades—to obtain title to a plot of land on which to build. Scores of different offices might be involved in the approval process, each requiring its own bribe and each insisting on its own waiting period. In some cases, the ownership of land is nebulous, with poor or nonexistent records and competing claims going back a century or more to when those countries were under colonial rule. Since you can't wait for twenty years to build, you might well decide to go ahead with construction in the hope that everything will eventually work out. But with such an informal arrangement, a bank may refuse to lend you the money to build: with no title to the land they would be afraid of losing their investment. So, you build a much smaller shop than you might have wished to build, and you pay the local mafia to protect your right to be there. To avoid attracting the attention of the tax police, who have the authority to interpret maddeningly vague laws as they please, you keep your business small and forego buying machines that would make it more efficient and profitable. You could spend your whole life in this type of shadow economy, never able to leverage the results of your hard-earned money. Every year, sometimes every day, is its own struggle and you feel very much on your own rather than a member of a society in which you have a stake, one that you would defend against those who would change it by force.

The obvious solution to this problem is to import a solid legal system that recognizes personal property and enables people to benefit from their accumulated capital, but this is much easier said than done. How do you go into a country and decide who actually owns what and who is illegally occupying land that belongs to someone else? More than that, how do you deal with cultures that have a different view of property than modern Western nations? For example, in many tribal societies land and much of the movable property is communal, belonging to the group rather than an individual. To insist that it be assigned formal ownership could destroy much of the social cohesion that derives from joint ownership. Here is a case in point: One African tribe used to build its villages in a circular arrangement, with the doors pointing inward toward a central court. They shared the results of their hunts and, except for a few personal items, tended to exchange gifts as a means of ensuring social equity. However, once they began to get a little money with which to buy Western goods, they began to fear losing them and before long began to turn their huts around so that the doors faced *outward*, away from the common court. Within a few years the social fabric began to disintegrate with increased levels of alcoholism and domestic violence. While private property is a fundamental right in Western society, it can cause problems when suddenly introduced into other cultures. Lastly, remember that some of those tribal societies are the same ones with vast stores of natural resources vital to the smooth running of the industrialized world. They cannot be ignored until they "grow up."

Problems arising from rapid changes to economic systems plague more than poor countries, as can be seen from the rapid rise of organized crime in the fledgling capitalist systems of Russia and many Eastern Bloc countries. During the early 1990s the term "business man" was nearly synonymous with "criminal" in Russia, partly due to the fact that it was theoretically impossible to run a completely legal business. This was a time when the taxes on some commercial enterprises exceeded gross income, meaning that anyone who made money was skirting the law. Added to this was the propensity of people in positions of power to engineer profitable selloffs of state property to themselves, their family, or friends or to divert foreign assistance into private bank accounts. It was estimated that as much as 75 percent of the aid money sent to Russia ended up in foreign bank accounts. Russian oligarchs became so wealthy that they engaged in bidding wars against one another for real estate on the French Riviera.

Even when the solution to an economic problem has a veneer of respectability, the results can be disastrous. The government of Zimbabwe decided to break the white monopoly on land, one that dated back to colonial days, by appropriating large white-owned farms, breaking them into pieces, and distributing them to black citizens. All well and good, one might say, except that the new residents were so hopelessly inept as farmers that the country went from a net exporter of food to a net importer. The economy went into a crashdive, with effects well beyond those directly affected by the land exchange. Unemployed farm workers flocked to the cities, only to live in squalor as they overwhelmed the already fragile municipal infrastructure. The government took harsh measures to reverse the migration, but this only exacerbated the situation. Fundamental changes in the land ownership system were required, but in this case the changes were done in such a way as to almost guarantee failure.

There are some seemingly obvious solutions to faltering economies that, upon a second or third look, begin to lose much of their initial attraction. For example, if the main problem in a resource-rich country is that rebels keep stealing the resources, claiming that they are fighting for the people when in reality they are enriching themselves, perhaps the solution would be to send more military aid to the central government to enable it to find and destroy those rebels. Sounds good, until that same military aid is used by the central government to attack a neighboring country with its own rich reserves of oil, diamonds, or timber. As has happened too often in the past, military aid can have the effect of keeping a tyrant in power far longer than might otherwise be the case, exacerbating the problem rather than reducing it. When designing economic measures to reduce the probability of mass violence, it is critical to put them into a total context and to pay careful attention to the particular situation of the recipient.

There are no easy remedies to the economic conditions that lead to mass violence. Until recently, we could largely ignore most problems simply because they were far away and had little effect on our lives or interests. We cared less about indigenous diseases in Africa before HIV/AIDS began to infect tens of thousands of Americans and Europeans. We could delay taking a stand on a civil war in Nigeria if it did not affect the price of oil. But if one of those far-off countries were to use its university biology lab to create its own biological weapon, then the situation would be different. We no longer have the option of standing by and watching others kill one another, confident that the effects will remain far distant from us and our loved ones.

So what *should* we do? How can we use the economic tools at our disposal to reduce the probability of mass violence? Despite all the ways that things can go wrong—misuse of aid and military assistance by the elite, to name but two of them—there are some success stories. The governments of several African countries, including Uganda and Ghana, responded to skepticism from international lending organizations and agreed to an unprecedented level of transparency in their national finances, enabling lenders to verify that their money was being used for the intended purpose. The results have been impressive, with Uganda in particular achieving growth rates near 7 percent for several years. Investments were made in critical infrastructure and there was hope that this country, which suffered so much under the harsh dictatorship of Idi Amin, might really turn itself around. The citizens of Uganda saw real improvements in their living conditions, raising their confidence in the central government and hence reducing the temptation to listen to rabble rousers who would destabilize the country for their own gain. Only when Ugandan involvement in regional wars began to sap the resources of the central government did the outlook begin to dim, but the improvements that have already been achieved are impressive. But here again we see the need for a holistic approach to aid, and an appreciation that economic measures must be coordinated with diplomacy. When a country like Uganda improves to the point where it is tempted by foreign adventures, that is the time to apply diplomatic pressure to get it back on the track of lasting reform. And, since the intended target of aggression is most likely also a benefactor of American aid, both sides of the conflict can be worked to the advantage of peace. However, these things do not just happen; they must be planned and have a priority just as high as education, health care, agricultural assistance, and other assistance goals. We must *work* at making and keeping the peace, keeping clear goals in mind.

There is an old saying: "Give a man a fish and he eats for a day, but teach him to fish and he eats for a lifetime." The same thing applies to international aid. Sending sacks of grain to feed a starving population soothes the consciences of rich populations, making them think that they are doing something about mass starvation, but what about spending a fraction of that money to improve agricultural yields by building irrigation systems and controlling devastating pests? Sometimes the most effective means of improving crop production is simply providing advice through agricultural extension services, inexpensive but incredibly effective. The Peace Corps and other organizations do just this type of thing, with the added benefit of creating lasting goodwill between the American volunteers and indigenous populations. There is no better way of showing that we really care about people than by working side-by-side with them, living in their villages, learning their languages, and helping them to improve their living conditions. Once again, the greatest long-term benefit from aid occurs from tackling the fundamental causes of problems rather than their symptoms, by thinking ahead to prevent a catastrophe before it occurs. Considered this way, aid is more than an altruistic handout to people who should be able to take care of themselves—it is a hard-nosed investment to prevent problems from occurring in the future, problems that may directly affect the United States.

Access to food is only one of the systemic causes of large-scale violence in poor countries. In the case of the Congo, one of the enabling factors behind rebel movements was their ability to hide in remote areas. Building better roads would have the dual advantage of providing a means for government forces to get to remote areas and getting goods to market. In Indonesia, rebel groups steal timber while it is en route to ports for sale. If better roads were available, this would be much more difficult. Roads would yield the dual benefits of improving the economic conditions of people in the interior and suppressing violent groups by removing their primary source of income. Providing a better communications system is another way to help development and reduce violence. In addition to the obvious business opportunities that it would create, it would enable problems to be reported in real time.

Countries that are heavily dependent on natural resources seem to be more prone to large-scale violence than countries with diversified economies. Gold and diamonds in African countries and timber in Indonesia were strong lures for rebel groups to try to get their share of the national treasure. To reduce this temptation, assistance could be provided to help wean the country from a heavy dependence on a single market. Tax incentives could be given to companies in developed countries to start small seed operations in potential trouble spots; an elaboration of this concept could even provide insurance in case things turn sour. Educational institutions could be supported to provide training for local people who would be employed by start-up companies. The economics of such concepts are attractive when one thinks of the massive amount of aid that currently disappears before it gets to its intended destination. Engaging the private sector in economic reform by backing start-up enterprises and funding training could be a bargain. However, we must be realistic: It would be foolish to start a high-tech semiconductor plant in a desperately poor country, one with no infrastructure and a population that would require years of education to be able to operate complex machinery. But it *would* be possible to start a clothing assembly plant, a furniture-parts fabrication facility, or other types of lower-end manufacturing endeavors that would provide a beginning for poor populations. These and other practical programs can have a long-term benefit to the people of the country involved and to those in nearby countries who would face lower risk from a more stable and dependable neighbor. Perhaps the greatest long-term benefit of these programs is that they give people hope, the confidence that they can improve their own lot without recourse to violence.

Sometimes the greatest progress in addressing critical issues in poor nations can be had by focusing on the little things that most directly touch people's lives, such as providing pumps and water purification equipment for villages, basic medical supplies for infirmaries, and simple school supplies. A broadband Internet connection would be a boon to a remote settlement, but it would be even better if the people in that settlement were able to read and understand what they saw on the screen. And any technology that we provide must carry along with it a dedicated and persistent supply chain of parts and repairs. Too often we have, with the best of intentions, provided equipment one year only to find it rusting the next for want of a battery or fuse. Focusing aid at the micro level encourages the creativity and energy of individual people, providing an example to others that they too could construct a better life for themselves and their families. Micro loans—some as small as $50—have had mixed but disproportionate success compared to some very expensive programs that have failed. Better to lose $50 on a hundred occasions than $50 million once.

Some of the most effective aid comes from outside government channels. Private organizations, such as Habitat for Humanity and Heifer International, have focused on providing enterprising people with a start on a better life, the former by building them a decent home in which to live and the latter by giving them livestock that can form the basis of a sustainable food supply or even a small business. Each year, my church sends a group of women to Mexico to build houses for poor families and each year they return with photos of beaming Mexicans who will be forever grateful to people who helped them get a leg up. Rather than paying rent, these people can now afford to send their children to school, transforming their lives and breaking the cycle of poverty that leads to frustration, crime, and violence.

How much is enough? While the United States gives more in absolute terms to the developing world than any other single country, it does not hold up its share as a fraction of gross domestic product. Whereas France contributes 0.41 percent of its GDP to needy countries and Great Britain gives 0.25 percent, the United States gives only 0.16 percent. International leaders have suggested that 0.7 percent of GDP is an appropriate figure for aid, a fair share of the developed world's riches and an investment in the avoidance of trouble later on. Out of a multitrillion-dollar budget, the United States spends more on weapons to protect us from a problem than on preventing that problem from occurring in the first place. Aid, properly focused and closely monitored, should be seen as an investment in our own future security rather than a handout. By focusing on how we can use economic tools to maintain the peace, we may well save money in the long run.

Following economist Hernando de Soto's argument that economic progress is often stymied by the lack of a system of laws that enables the accumulation of capital, an essential component of any international assistance program must include education on the legal infrastructure required to support a robust economy. Much has been learned in the developed countries about how land disputes can be settled, about the appropriate role of government in the oversight of industry, and about how to deal with corruption within the government itself. Sharing these lessons will multiply the effect of monetary aid many fold and will hasten the day when a previously poor country can stand on its own two feet. Here is a situation where economic measures must occur hand in hand with diplomacy; most countries will bristle when lectured on internal legal matters, which, in less developed societies, are often linked to politics and personalities. However, if we relate success stories in other countries and calm fears that reform will jeopardize the political system, we may be able to make progress.

Regulatory reform involves more than the receiving country—important stimuli to foreign development can be had through a prudent restructuring of American trade laws that sometimes discriminate against the few products that a developing country may be able to export. For example, if one of the few crops that a country can grow is cotton, then removing crippling import tariffs on raw cotton and processed textiles would encourage local industry, establish a viable tax base, and perhaps even improve the stability of the government and its ability to deliver services to its citizens. This reasoning can be taken to its most hardhearted extreme by calculating the net loss of jobs in the United States versus the cost of military intervention if the situation on the other side turns violent.

Even the best-intended aid and development programs could fail if the recipient country is unwilling to use them properly. It is unfortunate but true that some governments are so corrupt that the national treasury is little more than a checking account for the family and friends of the leadership. For example, while hundreds of thousands of people were starving in North Korea, the government ordered several hundred brand-new Mercedes-Benz automobiles. The factory, understanding the economic plight of the country, suggested that refurbished cars might fill the need at much lower costs, but the North Koreans insisted that the vehicles be new since they were intended as presents from the Dear Leader to his loyal supporters.

Sanctions are the other side of economic policy, the stick that complements the carrot of aid. When appropriately designed and applied, sanctions can hit corrupt government leaders where it hurts—in their pocketbooks. Economic sanctions on Iraq were designed to prevent Saddam Hussein from using his oil money to acquire more weaponry. While the blockade in the Persian Gulf was less than 100 percent effective, it certainly cut down on what would have occurred otherwise. And it had much less of an effect on the general population than Iraqi press reports would have you believe. Saddam claimed that sanctions were preventing urgently needed drugs from reaching his people, but he neglected to say that he was storing huge quantities of desperately needed medical supplies in warehouses, doling them out as favors to cronies, and keeping them from towns and regions that he thought disloyal. One can only think that the early imposition of sanctions on the Sudanese government would have put a halt to, or at least suppressed, the tragic violence in that country.

Midway between handouts and sanctions is conditional aid, money given with strings attached. To counter complaints of money disappearing into bureaucrats' pockets, strict transparency of government accounts can be insisted upon; regular visits to rural areas can ensure that aid makes it from the treasury in the capital to the people most in need. This worked in Uganda and it could work elsewhere. While it would be unrealistic to assume that one could instantly impose Western accounting standards in every country, there *are* ways to ensure that *most* of what is sent arrives at its intended destination. Sometimes a recipient country will object to intrusive requirements from donors, but in these cases one must ask why: Is it because of some real security issue, which is unlikely, or is it because it cramps the style of the leadership in diverting aid to its own use? If there is a security concern, perhaps we could work with the government to ensure that the required level of confidentiality is maintained while providing assurances to the donors. Flexibility can often help turn a no into a maybe. The United States has demanded increasing transparency into the use of its aid, appropriately so, since it is our taxpayers' money. This insistence, coupled with a program to help educate foreign leaders and their bureaucracies on how to manage money, has already paid off in some countries and will work elsewhere if pursued with determination.

There is an added benefit to transparency beyond just keeping government officials on the straight and narrow. Countries with corrupt governments are often havens for international crime, including human smuggling, drugs, and the laundering of money from illegal operations in other countries. By keeping better track of what money goes in and out of the country, it becomes more difficult for such criminal economies to persist. This also applies to arms smuggling, a critical factor in long-running civil wars and insurgencies. By making it harder for arms to be shipped to trouble spots, we could at least put the brakes on violence that could otherwise smolder for decades.

Some of these ideas are already being implemented in some form by the World Bank, the U.S. Agency for International Development, the United Nations, and other organizations. None of them are sure-fire, no more than any new technology is guaranteed to work or any new drug is guaranteed to be free of all side effects. But for the same reasons that we invest in new inventions and pharmaceuticals, we should be willing to invest in new economic programs. It is often cheaper to *prevent* a problem than to deal with it after it has become serious.

What is *not* being done and what is urgently needed is to focus our economic tools on *reducing the probability of mass violence*. We direct money to reducing child mortality, cutting HIV/AIDS infection rates, and eliminating malaria and other preventable diseases, so why not direct money to reduce another killer—mass violence? We plan almost every other aspect of our national programs, so why not construct a conscious economic policy that has as one of its goals the reduction of conflicts that kill hundreds of thousands of people? If we are willing to spend millions to feed people during a famine, to help them rebuild their country after a natural catastrophe, why not spend at least a fraction of that amount to prevent an equal number of deaths from war and genocide? From a ruthless cost-benefit standpoint, we should be *more* willing to make such investments, since, while we can't do much to stop an earthquake or a tidal wave, we *can* affect those things that are brought about by human decisions and are subject to change. Twice as many people died in the Rwandan genocide as in the tsunami that struck the western Pacific in 2004. More than *ten* times as many died in the Congo civil wars. We should certainly continue to help when disaster strikes, but we should pay equal attention to preventing *human-made* disasters.

One of the challenges of crafting economic programs to reduce the probability of mass violence is that they need to be implemented in a holistic sense. It would be foolish to shower aid on a corrupt government that would funnel the money into the Swiss bank accounts of its elite. It would be equally foolish to provide aid without helping to create a workable financial infrastructure that guarantees the property rights of the people. Some countries are anxious to get just this kind of help. Others are less so, but just as economic aid can serve as a stimulus to reform, so too can conditions on aid serve as sticks to induce bad rulers to change their ways.

We need to supply both the means—money—and the tools—financial systems—to enable a country to develop its own resources and lessen its dependence on foreign aid in the future. We must recognize cultural factors that might inhibit the instant acceptance of property systems that run counter to tradition. There is no instant solution to the set of economic conditions that leads to violence, but that doesn't mean that we should stand by and do nothing. During the cold war, ideology was a central criterion for helping other countries. Those that promised to stay out of the Soviet sphere of influence were rewarded and those that sided with Moscow were shunned or, even worse, intentionally destabilized. Now that the cold war is over, we can relax this political test in favor of a more rational investment in the future.

Economic tools can play a vital role in the reduction of terrorism. Implicit in all the ideas described above is the creation of hope for those who might otherwise feel that they have nothing to lose by joining a violent group. People who are busy getting on with their lives, who see a future for themselves and their families, and who believe that they at least have a chance at bettering themselves through their own efforts are much less likely to engage in mass violence.

Each of us can exert some influence on economic policy. Nike and Starbucks both felt the heat when activists began to expose their exploitation of workers in other countries, exploitation that could have led to animosity toward the United States. These companies improved their treatment of their foreign employees and turned these improvements into a sales pitch for their products. In today's global economy, buying a pair of sneakers can be a statement of your national security policy.

NINE ‖ **military capability to make and keep the peace**

Let him who desires peace prepare for war. —FLAVIUS VEGETIUS RENATUS

A red sun was setting behind a grove of desert palms, taking with it the scorching heat of a summer day in Baghdad. I was standing on the rooftop terrace of a small guesthouse on the grounds of Saddam Hussein's lake palace, about to pin Bronze Stars on three soldiers assigned to the Defense Threat Reduction Agency. These men had been among the first to enter Iraq in April 2003, and had endured months of sand, bugs, gunfire, and more sand. Their job was to be just behind, or occasionally just ahead of, the front line of advance looking for the tell-tale signatures of Iraq's rumored weapons of mass destruction. The fact that their job was technical in nature was lost on the Iraqis who shot at them just as they did at any other American in uniform. As the director of DTRA, I was in Baghdad to visit the hundred or so people assigned there from the agency, to make sure that they had everything they needed and that they were being well cared for by the larger army unit to which they were attached.

During my visit, we walked through one after another of the numerous palaces that Saddam and his sons had built for their amusement, palaces now taken over by coalition forces. Here were the blackened ruins of a theater that was bombed in the hope that Saddam was present; at the last minute he decided to do something else and dozens of underlings died in his place. There was the conference room familiar from television reports; I stood where Saddam had stood and felt a chill of history as I remembered that the fates of hundreds of thousands of lives were decided at that very spot. Everywhere there was the grotesque mimicry of an insecure tyrant—the chandeliers were plastic, the gilt was plastic, the huge wall reliefs were plastic—it was all for show, a cheap knockoff of luxury that fooled only those who knew no better.

As someone who has always treasured books, I was saddened to see the main library of the Iraqi Nuclear Center sacked, books and papers littering the floor of a building that had obviously been lovingly maintained in years before. However, in the basement of that same library, we found the room where the Iraqis stored the records of their nuclear weapons program, records now reduced to a heap of black ash and twisted metal. Not one shred had survived an inferno intended to destroy every trace of a program that the national leadership steadfastly denied existed. Did Iraq have nuclear, chemical, or biological weapons? We now know that it didn't, but we also know that it was only a matter of time, never far from the top of the list, with plenty of capability kept in reserve for the right moment.

I have spent most of my life working to ensure the national security of the United States, but I have usually done so from the security of an office in the United States. The men on whose chests I pinned Bronze Stars had left their families, journeyed far, and lived under the most demanding conditions to find and destroy any chemical, biological, or nuclear weapons that Saddam's regime might have begged, borrowed, or stolen. To stand atop that building pinning medals on three brave men was one of the proudest moments of my career.

We are a potentially violent species. To lay down our weapons in the hope that others will do likewise would be as foolish as disbanding our police forces in the hope that criminals would cease preying upon peaceful citizens. Most people would agree that we need some military capability. The question is, what *type* of military is best suited to address the challenges of the future. The cold war is over, but we face new threats from regimes seeking weapons of mass destruction and from international terrorism. We may not face thousands of Soviet tanks in Europe, but our military forces will likely be called upon to perform peacekeeping and counterinsurgency operations and protect our interests and allies around the world.

Experience teaches us valuable lessons. Unfortunately, the next war is usually quite different from the previous one. In past centuries, such a backward look was less of a problem since you could usually see a threat coming. It took weeks or months for the other side to mobilize its army, and we usually had a pretty good idea of what equipment we would come up against in combat. Today, ballistic missiles can deliver weapons across the globe in less than an hour. International couriers deliver packages in less than a day. We need to think ahead—well ahead—about how we would respond to a future crisis.

Few people think that the United States is in danger of attack by another nation-state. No country or combination of countries has sufficient force to win against the American military. Yet we continue to spend an enormous amount of money—more than $450 billion in 2005—on our national defense. Why? Wouldn't we be better off reducing our military expenditures, using those funds for urgent domestic programs or foreign aid, or to pay down the national debt?

Perhaps not. Our investment in defense is our strategic insurance policy. By spending this money we avoid even the smallest possibility of being drawn into a peer-to-peer war that could cause catastrophic damage to our country and much of the rest of the world. It is expensive, and we should always be on the alert for ways to reduce costs, but the alternative may be even more expensive.

However, our supremacy on the battlefield creates its own set of problems. Potential adversaries understand that they could never defeat the United States in a "fair" fight, so will they choose other means, including terrorism, guerrilla warfare, and maybe even the use of weapons of mass destruction? While our conventional forces still play a vital role in preventing large-scale conflict between nations, we need to pay attention to the evolution of the other threats against us and respond accordingly. All of our firepower may be of little avail if the enemy is a young woman with a bomb under her clothing. Attacking a crowd of civilians because we think that they harbor terrorists or insurgents could make peacekeeping even more difficult. And invading a country, for whatever reason, carries enormous costs in lives, money, and international good will. We need to be very smart in deciding whom we attack and how.

Smart is the operative word. I believe that the single most important factor affecting future military success—something more important than stealth or speed or explosive force—is accurate intelligence. We already have enough firepower to destroy every potential target on the face of the earth—force alone is no longer the sole arbiter of victory. The problem is that we don't know where to apply that force to best effect; we don't know how to recognize a problem early enough to take care of it when it is small, before it becomes nation-threatening. The old adage "Knowledge is power" is truer every day:

if we know where a threat lives, we can destroy it, but if we don't know where it is or, worse, don't know that it exists, then even the most powerful nuclear weapon won't save us.

The United States has suffered a series of stunning intelligence failures: from the collapse of the Soviet Union to the nuclear tests of India and Pakistan, from the *absence* of weapons of mass destruction in Iraq to the *presence* of a nuclear weapons program in Iran. Despite spending around $40 billion per year on intelligence gathering and analysis, we still seem unable to predict critical events. We have constellations of spy satellites that can see into almost every nook and cranny in the world, listen to any conversation, and sense minute concentrations of telltale chemicals that might be indicative of nefarious activity. We have legions of analysts toiling away in tiny cubicles, mining terabytes of data in hopes of uncovering that one gem that will earn them a spot on the president's briefing the following day. Yet after all this effort, we continue to miss the big picture by focusing exclusively on the details.

That is the problem. When you look at a forest through a high-powered telescope you see the details on each of the leaves rather than the whole forest. Modern intelligence is focused on gathering a plethora of little secrets; its masters are always wary of letting too many of those secrets assemble in the same place for fear that the "sources and methods" by which they were found might be discovered and the leak plugged. Almost no one, beyond the president and a very few others, has access to everything, so someone is almost always wrong when he or she says that they have "looked at all the intelligence data" in coming to a conclusion. We have come to confuse *information* with *secrets*, thinking that the only thing worth knowing about a potential adversary must be classified as tip-top secret, preferably obtained with the latest high-tech spy satellite or clandestine operation. Sometimes we are so focused on what is secret that we fail to see what is right out in the open.

My favorite illustration of the failure of this approach is the shock that ran through the intelligence community when, in 1998, India conducted a rapid sequence of nuclear weapons tests. In fact, we should have expected the test, since the BJP had written in their newspaper that, if they were elected, they would conduct a nuclear test. Our satellites told us that they were up to something, but there were only a few harried analysts assigned to the project and, ultimately, there was no one on duty to look at the final incriminating pictures. Just before the test, one of our diplomats had dinner with an Indian counterpart, who confidently told him that India was not about to set off a nuclear explosion. Alas, our informant may not have been on the list of people who actually knew anything about the Indian nuclear weapons program, so our first indication of the explosion was a jump on a seismometer. That was followed by a triumphant announcement in the Indian press and a less triumphant condemnation by many countries around the world, including the existing nuclear powers. We were shocked—but so too were the Indians, who wondered what they could possibly have done to make their intentions more obvious. We were looking for detail and we missed the forest for the trees.

Iraq was an intelligence failure of even greater proportion. I have been criticized by some of my colleagues in the defense community for saying this. My reply is this: If Iraq wasn't an intelligence failure, then I would like someone to explain to me what such a failure would look like so that I would be sure to recognize it next time. When I was director of DTRA, I was briefed several times on the "indisputable proof" that the Iraqis were building hundreds or thousands of centrifuges for the purification of weapons-grade uranium. I saw sketches of aluminum tubes that were purchased in great secrecy, tubes made of such fine aluminum and machined to such exacting tolerances that they could have but one use and one use only: nuclear weapons development. I remember asking if there were any other applications for such tubes, say, in the oil industry or in some other weapons system. No, I was told, no refinery used them and Iraqi rockets had a different diameter than the suspect tubes. (This turned out to be false.) And besides, my adviser continued, it would be wasteful to demand such expensive tolerances for simple artillery rockets. Around and around we went until, respecting the supposed superior knowledge of the intelligence community, I accepted the prevailing view that Saddam Hussein really did have an active program for developing weapons of mass destruction and it was only a matter of time before he had a working nuclear device.

I should have been a bit more suspicious when, at a meeting at the White House to discuss the information that Secretary of State Colin Powell would take to the United Nations, I was surprised to see very little hard evidence on the table. Almost everything discussed at that meeting had already been in the newspapers, although I was reminded the information in the press was "unconfirmed" and thus lacked the official stamp of a genuine intelligence product.

Things didn't get much better after that. During the war, I received reports of looting in the main nuclear materials storage site at Tuwaitha, just south of Baghdad. After the Iraqi troops fled, the local residents promptly broke into the compound, convinced that such a well-guarded facility must contain something worth stealing. What they found was a set of big plastic drums containing a yellowish powder (a uranium compound), a powder that they deemed of no value and dumped out on the ground. They wanted the containers to store water and milk. Since my troops were in Iraq to prevent WMD materials from falling into the wrong hands, such a report of looting at a nuclear facility was alarming to say the least, and I immediately called my counterpart in the intelligence community to ask for an opinion. "Only a rumor," he replied dryly. "We haven't had time to confirm it." But by then I was watching it live on CNN.

On another occasion, my commander in Baghdad called home to report that he had just taken his unit into a dangerous area to look at what turned out to be a parking lot. It was on the official list of sites that were suspected of harboring a WMD production plant but, after checking and rechecking his GPS unit and maps, he found only broken asphalt. We later learned that the building in question had been torn down the year before, but when I confronted the intelligence community with this information, I was adamantly told that such a mistake was impossible—my people must have gone to the wrong location. In fact, the photo that was the basis of the inspection was over two years old and was not updated prior to the invasion. Not to repeat *that* mistake, when an Iraqi tipped off one of my agency's soldiers that there might be something worth looking at just a quarter of a mile from where they were standing, we were told to wait until a satellite photograph could be taken to "confirm" the site.

I relate these stories to point to two fundamental problems that impede our ability to anticipate and respond to world events. First, the community spends too much time looking for *secrets* in dark corners and too little time looking for *information*, some of which can be found in broad daylight. As in the case of the Indian nuclear test, we discounted perfectly valid information because it came from a source outside the supersecret inner sanctum of the intelligence community. It's certainly true that not everything that you read in the newspapers is gospel, but it's also true that even some of the most coveted and protected secret sources can feed us wrong information, either through our own mistakes in interpretation or because the other side has planted erroneous data for us to find. Sometimes personal ego and attachment to pet theories can blind even the hardest-working intelligence professionals to facts staring them square in the face.

In my opinion, the second root cause of intelligence failures is that we have lost the sense of quality and scholarship that characterized analysis during the cold war. In the 1980s and early 1990s, I worked with analysts who had spent decades looking at what the Russians were doing. They knew every photograph, every name, every intercepted conversation there was to know. When new information became available, they could put it in context, occasionally sounding the alarm but more often noting that it was consistent with ongoing activity. And, most important, they were willing to say "I don't know" when they were stumped by a new development. Today, we have analysts with little experience in what they are analyzing, making it difficult or impossible for them to make sense of an isolated fact. Fixing this will take time and a dose of that most difficult to obtain quantity in Washington, patience.

It is not only institutional memory that seems to have slipped through our fingers over the past decade; we are also critically short of the type of technical expertise required to accurately interpret increasingly sophisticated weapons technologies. Twenty years ago, we could hire a retired air force test pilot and get a professional opinion on a new Soviet fighter jet. Today we need people who can assess the dangers of gene splicing, laser isotope separation, and molecular designs for chemical weapons. Is that research institute ordering a piece of equipment for purely peaceful purposes or is there quite a different intent? Some of the people tracking the most worrying developments in the world, such as nuclear weapons proliferation, have little or no technical expertise in the subject and are hard-pressed to make heads or tails of what they are seeing. They rely on consultants, occasional conversations, and what they read in the papers.

One of the timeless complications of intelligence analysis is that it involves (and requires) the *human element*. Satellites are good at seeing tanks and missiles, but they are notoriously bad at seeing into the changeable minds of people. In our data-centric, project-oriented culture, where everything is supposed to be measurable and predictable, we forget that life-or-death decisions can sometimes depend on the mood of one person. Also, the response of someone from a different culture can be very different from what we might anticipate based on our American values. In order to anticipate future threats, we urgently need to know more than just *what* people are doing; we need to understand *why* they are doing it, so that we can develop more effective means of convincing them *not* to do things that are damaging to us or to themselves. We need to know not just what they are *capable* of but also what they actually intend to *do* with that capability. Americans love definite answers provided by technology, and we sometimes forget that it is people, with all their frustrating ambiguity and perverseness, who decide most of what happens.

Intelligence, properly vetted, can help us see problems far enough in advance that we can try to construct a nonviolent solution, or at least a solution with a minimum of violence. But we shouldn't allow ourselves to be lulled into the illusion that, with only the right investment of time, people, and money, we could develop a perfect situational awareness of the whole world. There *is* no "perfect" view of the world, if for no other reason than that the world is constantly changing and individual human decisions can have profound effects on events.

Admitting that we might not know everything is sometimes as important as correctly interpreting those facts that are available to us. Suppose you thought that you had perfect information about the future of a particular stock. You did all the research, checked out the competitors, validated the company's financial plan, and everything told you to buy, buy, buy. Two weeks later, you discover that the product made by the company in question has a previously unknown flaw that will be costly to repair, greatly reducing the profit potential. Were you wrong to invest? No, because all the information at your disposal told you that this was going to be a great investment. But you might have hedged your bets by purchasing a balanced portfolio rather than a single stock. The same reasoning holds with intelligence—it is an *indicator* that can help you plan a balanced approach to the future, but, as with any other activity, we must learn to deal with uncertainty in assessing opportunities and threats.

With events happening faster and faster and their consequences becoming ever more serious, it is imperative that we fix the problems in the intelligence community so that we can have best warning of future trouble. We can then use all the tools at our disposal—including the full range of diplomatic and economic options—to mitigate the danger short of violence. But there may come a time when an imminent threat can't be stopped by any means short of force. The question then becomes, how *much* force should be applied? Uncertainty over future threats argues for a spectrum of capabilities from quick-reaction special forces that can do surgical strikes to heavy armor and mechanized infantry that can capture and hold territory. One does not replace the other—each has a role to play in keeping, or making, the peace.

Just like everything else, military technology is constantly changing. During medieval times, kings sought refuge in stone castles that were large enough and strong enough to withstand any but the most determined sieges. With the introduction of the cannon, once-impregnable walls were no longer a defense and they were simply abandoned in favor of open-town plans and mobile armies that could meet the foe far from home. Centuries later, speed was the be-all and end-all of fighter aircraft—moving many times the speed of sound was deemed essential to catching or evading the enemy. Today, speed is less of a factor than stealth and the ability to evade detection.

What weapons do we need to defend ourselves, to make and keep the peace in the future? The Pentagon has a major effort underway to answer this question, fully aware that an ever-changing world situation and the advance of technology require major adjustments in both equipment and the tactics that will govern the use of that equipment on the battlefield. Some existing weapons systems, such as large aircraft carriers that can maintain a presence in distant waters for months at a time, will continue to play a vital role for decades. New systems, such as unmanned aerial vehicles, will play an important function in providing reconnaissance and even combat capability with lower risks to American forces. Military technology has never remained the same for very long and we can expect it to continue to evolve to meet future requirements.

Advanced technology provides a key advantage to American fighting forces. By having better weapons, we can have fewer of them and still win any battle, any time. No one understood this better than Rear Admiral Jay Cohen, previous head of the Office of Naval Research (ONR). Jay supported an array of science and technology that would make any university president envious. Always moving at lightning speed, he jumped from radio astronomy to electric guns, from biodetectors to batteries, understanding that the country's best defense is to remain one step ahead of the competition. Jay had people stationed around the world, including in such unlikely places as Vietnam and Chile. He figured that there were smart people everywhere and he wanted their ideas. Closer to home, ONR helped fund the technology that Robert Ballard used to find and explore the wreck of the *Titanic.* In his lectures, Ballard emphasized that his expeditions were a great way to get young people interested in oceanography, but Jay privately admitted that he had "other applications" in mind for the technology. Somewhere down the line those unique sensors and cameras will find their way into navy ships. Those who see the Pentagon as a paragon of paralysis never met Jay, or many others like him, people who are not satisfied unless they are pressing against the next horizon.

The Gulf wars demonstrated the amazing precision with which the United States can deliver weaponry. After being told (in jest) to fly a cruise missile through the window of a building, a controller asked, "Which window, sir?" But some targets are so hard that they can sustain a hailstorm of missiles, bombs, or shells and still survive. More and more countries are learning the lessons of the Gulf wars and putting their crown jewels deep underground, in hardened bunkers or even under mountains. Such facilities, which sometimes include nuclear, chemical, or biological weapons production facilities, can only be confidently destroyed with nuclear weapons.

It may seem paradoxical that the most advanced military nation in the world, one without any serious competitor, still thinks that it needs nuclear weapons to defend itself. However, nuclear weapons represent the twenty-first century equivalent of Teddy Roosevelt's "big stick," a stick so big that there is no place safe enough to hide after an attack on our vital interests. Nuclear weapons are the modern manifestation of a phrase that the British used to cast on the side of their cannon: "The king's final argument." Nuclear weapons are final—there is no further argument.

I believe that nuclear weapons will continue to be important in assuring our national security. Should we disarm, we can never be sure that some other country hasn't kept a few in secret to use as a threat later on. However, I also believe that there is little reason for us to keep the large stable of very high yield, very destructive nuclear weapons that we had during the cold war. They are relics of an age when the precision of a missile was so poor that we needed a very big bang to assure ourselves of taking out a very hard target. Today, very few targets require more than 10 percent of the yield of a modern strategic warhead. Moreover, many of the missions that we used to assign to nuclear weapons—such as destroying mobile missiles carrying nuclear warheads—can now be achieved with a conventional weapon if it is delivered with high precision.

Being at the U.S. Strategic Command (STRATCOM) in the late 1990s was like walking down memory lane—the cold war was over but you would hardly have known it from some of our discussions. When, in a paper entitled "Nuclear Weapons in the Twenty-First Century," I proposed replacing some of the nuclear warheads on our missiles with nonnuclear ones, I was ridiculed. My peers on the STRATCOM Strategic Advisory Group were dedicated to maintaining the existing stockpile of nuclear weapons, and they produced chart after chart to demonstrate that conventional weapons were little more than firecrackers compared to "real weapons."

However, all this began to change with the arrival of Admiral Richard Meis on the scene in 1998. Tall and silver-haired, with a good sense of humor, but 100 percent Navy, Rich could have been typecast as a Hollywood admiral. He quickly picked up the arcane details of nuclear strategy and, rather than just listen to his advisers, he began to chart his own course for STRATCOM. He was convinced that if Strategic Command didn't change with the times it would become irrelevant, not something that any four-star officer would like to contemplate of his new charge. He initiated a series of studies to see what might be achieved with lower-yield, higher-precision, and he wouldn't take no for an answer. Slowly the ship began to turn. And, thankfully, he livened up what were sometimes stultifying official dinners by having his favorite song, "Bad to the Bone," played by the military band brought in for entertainment.

Meis was succeeded by Admiral James Ellis, who pushed even harder to get Strategic Command out of the Dark Ages when he took over in 2002. Within a year, he transformed STRATCOM into one of the most innovative organizations in the military. Ellis didn't see weapons as ends in themselves, to be maintained "just in case" we needed them. He focused on what missions he had to perform and only then asked what weapons were necessary for success. By the time he retired, Ellis could explain why we needed which nuclear forces better than anyone that I knew.

The commitment to reshape our strategic forces now goes all the way to the top. When the Pentagon sent a memorandum to President Bush recommending a larger number of nuclear weapons than he thought necessary, he picked up his pen, crossed out the numbers, and sent the memo back with his handwritten instructions.

There is a strong lobby against building any new nuclear weapons, a position that I find unfathomable since the alternative is to keep an aging stockpile of cold war dinosaurs that are much more destructive than required. Still more baffling is the argument for a continuum of capability from conventional nonnuclear bombs to nuclear weapons, the idea being that there should be a smooth transition between the largest nonnuclear weapon and the smallest nuclear weapon. I could not disagree with anything more strongly. The destructive force of the largest nonnuclear bomb is equal to about 20 tons of high explosive, easily capable of destroying a neighborhood. A typical strategic nuclear weapon has a destructive energy measured in *hundreds of thousands of tons* of high explosive, easily capable of destroying an entire city. Even a "small" nuclear weapon has a yield of *thousands* of tons of high explosive. Since nuclear weapons are the only weapons that could inflict serious losses on our forces, I believe that the United States should create an ever widening chasm in perceptions of conventional and nuclear weapons. We should do everything in our power to create the image that nuclear weapons are different, that an awesome threshold is crossed when one is used. I would like to say that this is altruistic pacifism, but in reality it is just good military strategy. It is in our best interest to keep any battle firmly planted on the conventional weapons plain, where we are sure to win. Our use of a nuclear weapon would send the message that it's acceptable to use a nuclear weapon against us— and that's the last thing that our generals and admirals should want to hear.

Not every future military operation will involve defeating an enemy on the battlefield. Rather than conquering the country, our goal in many cases will be to separate warring factions long enough for the politicians to sort things out. Until the invasion of Iraq, some military leaders saw peacekeeping as a peripheral duty, necessary in the interval between winning the war and returning home to yellow roses and parades. It is now clear to everyone that peacekeeping will be as important to ultimate success as the destruction of enemy forces. Just as we need to complete the transformation of our military to emphasize the right force for the mission, so too do we need to recognize the importance of knowing how to operate in noncombat situations in which words are as potent as bullets and a pallet of food is more valuable than a howitzer. This is not the touchy-feely side of military occupation, but a hard-headed recognition that we will always be outnumbered when we are the foreigners in another country. We need the help of the locals to make and keep the peace.

The fight against global terrorism requires similar changes in how we organize and deploy our forces. As we have found in the hunt for terrorist leaders in Afghanistan, it is exceptionally difficult to find one or a few people when they are determined to remain hidden, especially when sympathetic tribesmen are willing to hide them. Military force was effective at eliminating terrorist bases of operation, a case of a fixed set of targets whose destruction was easily achieved. And soldiers on the ground are essential to searching rugged terrain for terrorists and their caches of weapons. However, at the most elemental level, terrorism is a social problem more than a military mission. It is only by looking at the root causes of why people choose to engage in violent actions against innocent civilians that we can hope to make significant progress toward its eradication. The role of the military in fighting terrorism is one of attempting to put the problem back into the box after it has manifested itself. Far better to prevent it from happening in the first place.

Just as we need to integrate our economic policies with our encouragement of democracy around the world, so too do we need to integrate our military strategy into a coordinated plan to reduce the probability of mass violence. By the time that the last coalition soldier leaves Baghdad, the war in Iraq may cost upward of $1 *trillion*, not counting the tragic loss of life on both sides. Not even the United States can afford to use military force as the preferred solution to international problems. More than ever, we need a comprehensive national policy that uses all of the tools at our disposal—diplomatic, economic, and military—in a focused manner to reduce the probability of mass violence.

TEN | **the necessity of hope**

> The boundaries of the possible in the
> moral realm are less narrow than we think;
> it is our own weaknesses, our vices and
> our prejudices that limit them.
> —JEAN-JACQUES ROUSSEAU

My high school history course included the usual description of World War II, its causes and effects. This was an interesting period for my friends and me since we had watched a seemingly endless stream of war movies during our formative years. We were used to seeing people killed, at least on film, and we had what was then a typical interest in the history of the war and particularly the military hardware that was used to fight it. We had all assembled plastic models of warplanes and warships, played with toy soldiers in the backyard, and heard stories of our parents' wartime experiences. War seemed familiar, and at times even glamorous.

On one day that I will never forget, my history class consisted of a film on the Holocaust. It was a grainy black-and-white affair, put together from German footage, absent any narrative, which would have been superfluous anyway in the face of the horrific scenes that followed relentlessly one upon another. I had never even imagined that such inhumanity was possible. I had nightmares for weeks afterwards, waking up in the middle of the night with the images of that film fresh before me. It was one of the most traumatic events of my life. Even today, if images of those camps are shown on television, I must look away or even leave the room. My friend Walter Reich, the first director of the National Holocaust Museum, has made a standing offer to take me through the powerful exhibits there, but I have never been able to bring myself to accept. As someone of German descent, my heart cries out in shame that anyone, let alone anyone even distantly related to me, could commit such crimes. I have no pride in this cultural heritage, and I found my only trip to Berlin disturbing in a way that I still cannot put into words.

Statistics fail utterly to represent the extent of the suffering in the Holocaust. In my mind, there were not 6 million deaths but 6 million individual people who had lives and loves, hopes and dreams. Their future was wrenched from them not by a natural catastrophe or some savage group lacking in civilization, but by one of the most advanced nations that the world has ever known. I cannot comprehend the number of people killed—I can only think of each face, each voice, and the look in the eyes of these people as they were led to their deaths.

There was a time when people in developed countries could rest behind massive armies and navies, genuinely concerned about cases of genocide and warfare that occurred in distant parts of the world, but comfortable that those tragedies were far away. There was an argument, buttressed by the international order that arose following the Treaty of Westphalia, that civilized nations should avoid interfering in the affairs of other civilized nations. It was this desire to avoid foreign entanglements, to have other people solve their own problems, that delayed the entry of the United States into both world wars of the twentieth century. Certainly we could have intervened sooner, perhaps saving millions of lives in the process, but we saw those conflicts as the latest episodes in a long series of European squabbles, which were, in effect, not our fight.

Human misery, it seems, is insufficient to cause us to risk American lives. It is only when our national interests are at stake that we are galvanized into action. One need only contrast the cases of the Iraqi invasion of Kuwait with the several foreign incursions in the Congo to see that economic interest usually trumps humanitarian need. While there is no disputing the carnage caused by the Iraqis and the illegitimacy of their attempted annexation of what they called "Iraq's nineteenth province," the number of Kuwaiti deaths was a tiny fraction of the 4 *million* people who have died in the Congo. And, lest the Congo be somehow seen as an isolated case, one need only think of the genocide in Rwanda, Cambodia, the Balkans, and other places to appreciate the stark reality that, for all our avowed altruistic civility, we still seem to weigh costs and benefits in a remarkably hard-hearted manner.

The luxury of turning a blind eye to the suffering of people far away is coming to an end, not because we are becoming more moral, more ethically conscious of our responsibility to our fellow human beings, but because the very same personal interest that goaded us into action in Kuwait can be applied to more and more cases around the world. No longer can we limit our fear to the massive nuclear arsenal of the Soviet Union, confident that our conventional military forces could defeat any other threat that might arise. As we found on September 11, 2001, and again in our occupations of Afghanistan and Iraq, just having superior firepower does not guarantee security. In September 2001, we didn't know that the enemy existed until they struck, by which time it was too late. In Afghanistan and Iraq, we knew that the enemy was there, but we were unable to root them out fast enough or prevent others from joining their ranks. The most important element of our future military capability will not be guns or bombs but intelligence and understanding—knowing what threats we might face and how we might defuse those threats.

Fifty years ago, the technology required to construct nuclear weapons was restricted to a few nations. The Nuclear Nonproliferation Treaty of 1972 was put into place at a time when nuclear technology was so expensive and complex that it made sense for countries to agree to forgo its development in the hopes that others would do likewise. Rather than spend billions of dollars on uranium enrichment, missile technology, and the other accessories of nuclear status, it seemed better to take a nonnuclear pledge and leave nuclear weapons to the global giants who, it was supposed, would be unlikely to use them.

As we have seen over the past decade, the hope that countries will voluntarily limit their nuclear ambitions is fast fraying at the edges. North Korea continues to flirt with nuclear technology, both as a means of ensuring the continuation of its bizarre hermit regime and as a bargaining chip to extort foreign aid. Pakistani nuclear scientists apparently had no scruples at passing along nuclear weapons technology to whomever had the cash to pay for it. As I write this, Iran insists that it is pursuing uranium enrichment for "energy purposes" despite the fact that it sits on one of the world's largest supplies of fossil fuels. Also, Iran is pursuing enrichment to much higher levels than would be required for nuclear power. More and more, it is the will of the government, rather than cost or technical complexity, that determines whether a nation decides to cross the nuclear threshold. Even though the technical challenges are still great, if a country wants to become a nuclear state, it can most likely find a way to get there, quite possibly without other countries knowing about it.

If nuclear technology is still too expensive, a country or group could always turn to the tremendous advances in biotechnology for another class of weapons that could be equally destructive toward human beings. Scientists have already demonstrated and—for reasons that seem to defy common sense—published how one can use readily available materials to construct a disease that is resistant to all known treatment. While one of their goals was to alert society and the government to a new and frightening threat, they have also provided both the idea and the means to achieve it to anyone with a modest capability in molecular biology. It is entirely possible that the person or persons who sent anthrax to the office of the Senate majority leader could modify that anthrax to make the next attack much more deadly. Rather than an envelope sent through the post, they could choose a delivery method that would infect far more people with far greater effect.

The existence of large quantities of toxic chemicals in every industrial nation gives would-be destroyers a ready means of achieving their ends with almost no expense or technological proficiency. The effect of a massive release of toxic gas on a civilian population was demonstrated in a gruesome fashion on the night of December 3, 1984, when 40 tons of highly poisonous methyl isocyanate accidentally leaked from a Union Carbide pesticide plant in Bhopal, India. Within hours, over 3,000 people were dead, and over the ensuing years, more than 10,000 additional deaths have been linked to exposure to the gas. Hundreds of thousands of others still suffer from respiratory and other health problems.

Mass destruction can be wrought with much more primitive

technologies than nuclear, biological, or chemical weapons. Over 800,000 people were killed in Rwanda with weapons as simple as machetes and clubs. But the Rwandan government still used the technology at its disposal—national radio—to order and coordinate the killing.

We have the records of fifty centuries of warfare that amply demonstrate our ability to destroy on a wholesale level using whatever technology is at hand—from spears to stealth bombers. What is different today is the unprecedented number of countries and groups that have access to the ability to cause mass destruction and, thanks to stunning advances in communications and transportation, to act faster than we can think about a response. For the first time in our history, it is becoming too expensive to wait for a problem to manifest itself before we take action. No longer can a Roosevelt resist the pleadings of a Churchill, claiming that it is not his fight and that the democratic process that elected him would never tolerate spending American lives on foreign problems. Leadership has been thrust upon the United States. We abdicate that leadership at our own peril.

Are we by nature violent animals that are destined by our genes to commit ever greater acts of destruction? Is violence, including mass violence, hardwired into our brains in such a way that it cannot be eliminated without changing our very human nature? I think that we now have enough data to prove that it is not. Over the past century, we have come to know and understand ourselves as social animals better than we have during all of our history. We have probed deeply into the human brain to understand what motivates people to commit violent acts or to stand by while violent acts are committed. We have collected and analyzed the records of hundreds of civilizations, seeking to understand why some social systems seem to work well and others fail. For all of our fascination with technology, we have come to recognize that it can create as many problems as it solves. As we enter the twenty-first century, we are beginning to recognize that the most pressing security problems that we face are those associated with *people*. It is only by grappling with the root causes of terrorism, war, and genocide that we can avoid a future darker than any imagined by Orwell or Huxley.

Extensive studies have shown that human beings can indeed live in peace. There are a number of small societies around the world where violence is almost unknown, where any type of physical force is socially unacceptable. And there has been a steady decline in the homicide rate in more complex cultures as strong central governments have created legal systems that permit the resolution of differences short of individual violence and revenge. These are strong indications that, while human beings are *potentially* violent, under the right conditions this potential can be held in check.

However, the appalling carnage of war and genocide demonstrates that, under the wrong conditions, human beings can be incredibly violent. We are social animals who love to compete. We have a strong need to belong to groups, to base part of our identity on those groups, and to distinguish ourselves from people in other groups. This ability to alienate other human beings, combined with a drive to compete and show our superiority over them, has led to justifications of wars, genocide, and, more recently, to organized international terrorism.

Aristotle wrote that there are two kinds of laws: the laws of nature, which humans cannot change, and the laws of the city, which humans can change. Our greatest encouragement that mass violence might be controllable is that the worst of our abuses are a result of the social systems in which we live rather than a fundamental flaw in our human nature. And, since we invented those social systems, we can change them.

But how do we change the complex societies in which we live, societies that have evolved to solve the problem of thousands, millions, and now billions of people living in close proximity to one another? Aren't such social systems essential to life in the modern world? Yes, but to say that *violence* is an inevitable part of society is as groundless as saying that slavery is inevitable, or starvation, or preventable disease. Each of these was once considered a natural part of life, but each of them was (largely) overcome. Mass violence is no more inescapable than slavery. We invented the social systems in which we live, and we can change them.

But changing our society requires effort. Slavery did not go away on its own and we don't expect poverty and disease to magically disappear. We have to *make* it happen. As we approach the time when more nations, groups, and even individuals can wreak destruction on an unprecedented scale, it is imperative that we devote the same level of attention to mass violence as we do to other urgent social problems.

We have powerful tools at our disposal—diplomatic, economic, and military—that we can use to reduce the probability of mass violence in the future. We have found that democratic governments have lower domestic violence *and* international violence. We have tried numerous schemes for foreign aid and have identified factors that optimize it as a means for establishing stable, democratic, and peaceful societies. And we are getting a better understanding of the capabilities and limitations of armed forces in making and keeping the peace.

As much as we have learned about ourselves and the societies in which we live, there is still much that we need to learn. Since World War II, and even before, most of the research and development funded by the federal government has been focused on the physical sciences and engineering. While we must be careful to maintain ourselves at the forefront of technology—if for no other reason than that technology is the foundation of our modern economy—we need to begin an urgent program to expand our investment in the social sciences. After all, if *people* are central to the threats that we face in the future, then we should make every effort to improve our ability to interpret, and perhaps even to predict and modify, the behavior of *people*.

For example, we can better understand how small societies that were formerly plagued by incredibly high rates of violence made the transition to peace. While indigenous societies lack many of the social complexities of modern culture, that very simplicity allows us to focus on key factors that are common to all human beings. Clayton and Carole Robarchek investigated the Waorani of Ecuador, perhaps the most violent people ever encountered. More than 60 percent of all adult deaths among this tribe were due to violence, much of it locked up in endless cycles of revenge killings. Violence was deeply ingrained in their culture, which was very much an "every man for himself" enterprise. Old people were speared by their own grandchildren when they became too weak to search for food, and mothers abandoned their children during a raid on their village. Killing was considered a natural part of life. Yet, when presented with a different way of resolving disputes, the Waorani stopped killing one another in a remarkably short period of time. Extensive interviews conducted by the Robarcheks confirmed again and again that this formerly "bloodthirsty" people wanted to stop killing, but they lacked the tools to construct a new social order. Once those tools were presented by missionaries and government administrators, they were eagerly adopted, complementing rather than replacing the native culture by reducing unnecessary suffering. If the Waorani can change when presented with a better option, is it too much to think that we could, given all our knowledge and analytical capability? What else can we learn from other societies to guide us on our own path toward reducing violence?

We need to continue this work, but we also need to take it out of the halls of academia and put it to practical use. Our universities have enormous resources that can contribute to peace in the future and there is an urgent need to increase the level of support for this work. But we must also make sure that this information gets to policy makers and planners in a form that they can use. The Pentagon has long recognized the need to have physical scientists and engineers in the military. Today there is an equally urgent need to bring social scientists into the defense establishment to help us solve some of the seemingly intractable people problems that we face now and the even more difficult ones that we are sure to face in the future.

While we have a number of tools at our disposal to reduce the probability of future mass violence, they will be most effective only when we *coordinate* them. Economic measures can help stimulate democracy, and the threat of military force can be a potent way to get dictatorial regimes to the negotiating table. Admiral Thomas Fargo, former commander of the U.S. Pacific Command, calls this "building good governance," a holistic approach that includes multiparty democracy, a free press, and a legal system that gives people confidence that their interests will be heard in a fair manner.

Fargo was more than an admiral. As commander of all U.S. forces in the Pacific, he was responsible for American interests across more than 100 million square miles of oceans, islands, and continents. He and his staff got to know almost all the leaders and societies across the Pacific, and they were able to draw some general conclusions that would have been impossible for an ambassador in a single country. Perhaps more than any other person in the government, he was able to construct a global view based on direct experience with dozens of different countries and cultures.

Fargo saw that democratic governments were the best at meeting the needs of their people, but he also found that having a perfunctory vote every few years did not guarantee that more than one voice was heard, a fact evident in the near rubber-stamp reelection of governments in many parts of the world. True democracy requires more than one voice in government, preferably in a rough balance that prevents the ruling party from running roughshod over the interests of minorities. Representative governments with multiple branches ensure that there is always an opposition that will promote discussion and argument on the most important issues. Greater participation by ordinary citizens helps to counter the effects of special-interest groups, some of which are more intent on their own agendas than the welfare of the people.

Another part of Fargo's argument for a holistic approach to nation building is that there be a free press that can present different perspectives. If the ruling party controls everything that the people hear through state-run newspapers, radio, and television, then debate will be perfunctory at best and self-serving at worst. Here there is hope, for the seemingly unstoppable spread of cell phones, the Internet, and other forms of communication is making it harder and harder for governments to keep their citizens in the dark. People may choose what we consider to be the wrong sources from which to get their news, but at least they have a choice.

Finally, a coordinated approach to good governance must include the reform of the legal system argued for by economist Hernando de Soto. What is needed is a system of laws that respects property and encourages the development of business and society in a way that enables each individual to achieve his or her full potential while respecting the rights of others. This is much more than a profit motive, or a simplistic notion that by distributing its wealth a nation will somehow become more peaceful and less prone to internal or external conflict. Rather, it recognizes that a fundamental characteristic of human beings is that we want to improve ourselves—we have a restlessness that drives us toward new horizons. Kept in constructive channels, this restlessness can produce feats of brilliance in combating disease, increasing the food supply, and improving the conditions of life. Allowed to stray into destructive channels, social chaos and warfare can result in untold misery. A legal system that respects private property is basic to providing an outlet for individual ambition and in suppressing the temptation to use violent means to achieve an end. When people are confident that what they have will not be unfairly confiscated and when they think that, through their own peaceful efforts, they can improve their own lives and those of their children, then they are much less likely to go outside the law—including using violent means—to secure that future. Simply put, they have a stake in the game. Conversely, when people feel that the deck is stacked against them and that nothing that they can do within the system is likely to improve their lot, then the attraction of violent groups becomes much greater.

It is important to channel the inherent restlessness of the individual into productive channels; it is just as important to provide analogous opportunities for societies. There appears to be no long-term stability in human affairs, if for no other reason than societies are constantly being reinvigorated by new people and new technologies. Organizations appear to move either forward or backward and seem unable to remain static for very long. Our challenge is to provide a social order that provides an outlet for this collective drive, one that enables the energies of groups as well as individuals to be used to constructive advantage. The United States is now on its third dimension of expansion, starting with the geographic expansion typical of empires, shifting to industrial production, and then to development of the service and information economy. If we can provide peaceful and productive outlets for our creative energy, perhaps other countries can as well.

Some factors that influence mass violence are out of our control, such as changes in weather patterns that affect crop yields and dwindling oil reserves that drive up the cost of living in industrialized countries. It would do little good to ponder a theoretically brilliant social and political system that foundered on the rocks of natural catastrophes or resource limitations. When thinking about the world that we would like to create, we need to keep a sharp eye on what our planet will tolerate and support. The effect of industrial policy on the environment, the rate at which we deplete irreplaceable natural resources, and the equity with which we distribute such vital and finite resources as freshwater will all influence decisions involving war and even terrorism.

There are other constraints to action, particularly those related to the persistence of national and cultural trends. Cultures change very slowly and are remarkably immune to preaching; true change requires persistent effort. It took a long time—many decades—for democracy to take hold in the United Kingdom, France, and even in the United States, but that does not mean that we should delay in starting the process. We literally haven't a moment to lose.

The United States will likely encounter problems in the international arena even if democracy and free-market economics spread to every country in the world. Even democracies occasionally will take positions opposite to American interests. However, here is where the qualities of a true leader become apparent. A leader is not someone who always wins, who always gets his or her way, but someone who is able to reconcile differences so that progress is made toward the ultimate objective. The United States is the most powerful nation on Earth—we don't need to prove it every day. We can use our power as a reserve, enabling us to be flexible in dealing with other countries, confident that we could force the situation if necessary. Flexibility in this sense does not mean that we have to give up something or sacrifice our convictions. It simply means that we can be more strategic in thinking about when we will realize the returns from our investment. Policies and decisions made to boost short-term profits or ego might well result in the need to spend significant sums to later bail out a failed regime or to counter a hostile military threat.

Is there a counterargument to the notion that we should suppress, or even eliminate, mass violence? Do "small wars" serve as a pressure release to mitigate even greater catastrophe, their elimination a sure path toward the very type of global conflagration that we hope to avoid? The argument is plausible, but the facts say otherwise. History tells us that large wars are as likely to follow small ones as they are periods of relative peace, and that domestic violence is *more* likely to occur at the end of a war, when so many soldiers and citizens are used to seeing death and destruction, than it is during a period of peace. Moreover, the temptation to engage in preemptive warfare may prove too great for even the wisest leader and could hypnotize the weak one who becomes captivated by his or her own power and reputation. The benefits of war in reminding our species of the potential violence we are capable of are outweighed by the dangers of its escalation to the global scale with millions of casualties.

Our attitude to war on any scale must remain one of abhorrence and avoidance; all measures should be sought to avoid it and to divest it of that "glory" that encourages it and forgives its cruel excesses. Recognizing our tendency to violence is not a rationale or a justification for its pursuit. It would be as foolish to do this as it would be to encourage a drug addict to take his next dose. War is a byproduct of human nature, but one that we can and must resist, just as we resist other excesses that are destructive in the long run. However, there are times when it is necessary to use limited violence to prevent an even greater evil. To stand by while others suffer is to accept some of the responsibility for that suffering. Military force must always be a last resort, but to rule it out completely would be to encourage its use by others. Our history gives ample illustration of what happens when good people stand by while evil flourishes. Passivism cannot be an excuse for inaction, nor should violence be seen as a cure for violence. By staying focused on our goal of reducing the probability of mass violence we can find the middle road in a world where absolutes are few and far between.

I began this book with a set of frightening scenarios in which terrorists used weapons of mass destruction against American cities. How will the spread of democracy, the crafting of focused economic programs, and military preparations for future wars help prevent these types of attacks? Don't we need different policies to deal with countries and with terrorists? The fact is that the proliferation of weapons of mass destruction is beginning to blur the distinction between international warfare and terrorism. Today, terrorists can kill thousands, but the time is fast approaching when rogue nations and terrorist groups will have access to the same level of destructive potential as a major country. Our approach must be one of reducing *all* forms of mass violence, regardless of the size of the perpetrating organization.

We apply rigorous project planning to space launches, factory production, and just about every other activity that we value. Why can't we apply the same degree of rigor to making and keeping the peace? We could set goals, deploy resources, measure trends, and adjust our course as we learn new lessons. We could calculate return on investment—both the avoidance of military action and the gaining of new trade partners. Why, as Glenn Paige points out in his book *The Nonkilling Global Society*, should the elimination of violence not be as valued an academic and practical discipline as the preparation for war? Why shouldn't reducing the threat of mass destruction be a top national priority, one demanding the president's attention, a key component of our foreign policy and defense planning? A systematic and comprehensive approach that combines political, economic, and military components, one that is done with the same degree of determination that we apply to other national priorities, has enormous promise and will help to place the United States back where it should be, the shining beacon of hope to all humankind, an example of how nations should behave on the world stage, a true leader.

Given our violent history, does a determined effort to prevent mass violence have any chance of success? Why should we devote our time and treasure to what might be an unattainable goal? *Because we do not have a choice.* Either we get serious about mass violence— made all the more dangerous by the proliferation of weapons of mass destruction—or we trust to fate. Either we take action to identify the root causes of large-scale violence and put measures in place to address them, or we will be forced to deal with an increasingly complex set of situations that could rapidly get out of hand, causing destruction on an unprecedented scale. And because of the accelerating pace of events, either we put these measures in place *now* or we will be forever behind, dealing with consequences rather than prevention.

We are an imperfect species, but one with great promise. There is hope. If we can use the tools available to us to reduce the probability of mass violence, then surely our children's children will rise up and call us blessed.